A Λ

MW01286141

The Light Through My Tunnel

Overcoming Tragedy Through Courage and Faith

Mary Varga

A Memoir

Behold, I am doing a new thing. Now it springs forth. Do you not perceive it? Isaiah 43:19, paraphrased

Dedication

This memoir is lovingly dedicated to all of my family members. When tragedy strikes, the whole family is affected. All of our lives have been changed. Their love, compassion and support were crucial in my recovery.

. To my son, Andrew Daugherty. I couldn't be the mother I always dreamed of being, but he has been a light in my life since the day he was born. I'm so proud of the man he is becoming!

. To my father, Donald T. Varga, the patriarch of the Varga family. He has always been my hero and the one whose opinion matters the most to me.

. To all my siblings and their spouses. They're a large group! Dan, Kim, John, Tracy, Paul, Missy, Andrew, Ann, Todd, Julie.

. And to the next generation! Katie, Beau, Sam, Noelle, Tess, Jack, Max, Ben, Will, Charlie, Abbey, Jake, Lauren.

. And the start of another generation with soon-to-be-born baby boy Boyd.

This memoir is also in loving memory of my mother, Shirley Long Varga. She was always my number one fan and my role model for what a good, Christian family should look like. I wish so much that she could be here to be proud of me.

Acknowledgments

The Holy Spirit prompted me to share my story, but I want to thank Nancy Vinson, my friend in Little Rock, for first encouraging me to magnify the Lord with what He has done in my life. I couldn't have done this without the encouragement and literary expertise of Louisville Christian Writers. Special thanks goes to our president, Crystal Murray, Mary Gaskins, Harriet Michael, Joyce Cordell and my friend Lisa Prysock for their guidance and expertise; and Lisa, for holding my hand through the publishing process. You made this book come to life!

So many people helped make this book a reality. I'm grateful for my father, Don Varga, for being my memory and medical expert in the earlier chapters; Kim Aubrey for offering her journalistic skills for my book proposal; Michael Lattin, BMB Productions, for being willing to produce an outstanding book trailer to promote my memoir on social media; J. Baker Hill for his expert editing.

I want to give a special thank you to Bob Stobaugh. He was the Emergency Room R.N. who saw my accident and ran over to resuscitate me. Because of Bob, I am still here today to write and publish this inspiring story that includes his act of heroism!

50% of the profit from my book sales will go to the Brain Injury Alliance of Kentucky. It was BIAK who gave me a name in the brain injury community. They have been a help and encouragement to me...as they are to all those affected by brain injury.

Table of Contents

INTRODUCTION

On May 10, l997, I was in a car accident. The impact of the collision totaled my car and spun it around in its tracks. I sustained a traumatic brain injury (TBI), and lived to tell the story.

I continue to recover even as I write. The brain is an amazing machine that can learn all kinds of ways to do things. But even more awe-inspiring is the One who created our bodies and our brains. I will talk about my particular head injury throughout the book, but it is important to realize that every brain injury is different. Depending on what part of the brain is damaged, different consequences will result. Initial treatment for a head trauma is somewhat universal, but recovery is very individual. I can speak only to my specific circumstances.

Like brain injury, faith in God is an individual path. I found my faith growing stronger as I continued writing. Perhaps your faith is deeper. Wherever you are in your faith journey, I pray my story will prompt you to reflect on the Sovereign Power that controls our lives. The Lord is doing a special work in me. I stand humbled and filled with joy at what He is creating. My task is to let God be God and stop trying to control everything myself.

John 16:33 says, *"I have told you these things, that you may have peace. In this world you will have trouble. But take heart! I have overcome the world."* With the direction and loving compassion of our Lord, I have finally been able to make peace with my disabilities and use my experiences to bring comfort and inspiration to others.

You will see my frustration come out occasionally. *Why did this happen to me? I had so much!* Life, as I knew it, was over. I knew it was an accident, but this was so hard! I would not wake up tomorrow to see it go away. However, like Job, I refused to curse God and die. I believed the Lord had saved my life for a purpose. I have a new life with lots of new plans and dreams. I turn to the Lord continually to keep myself centered in that new life.

This *new* life did not happen smoothly. I am no stranger to the challenges that come with disabilities. I am no stranger to God's discipline: He has tested me, challenged me, and, more than once...put me in my place, yet He has always shown His love for me. Just like my earthly father, my Heavenly Father has the ability to make me a little nuts sometimes. It seems that I have been a resistant learner; He has to keep teaching me the same things over and over again.

I believe that dealing with suffering makes us better and stronger people. My perseverance, determination, and strength have grown exponentially since the accident. As my life continues, I am becoming one strong cookie!

I was raised in and continue to belong to the Roman Catholic Church. You will find symbolism and references to my Catholic faith throughout my story. You will also see my faith evolve throughout the book as I gain a deeper grasp of God's word.

My perspective on life, love, and the Lord evolves from the first chapter to the last. Writing this memoir has been very therapeutic for me. I have become more peaceful, compassionate, and forgiving. Perhaps I am finally catching some of those lessons that God has been showing me again and again.

On my high school senior retreat, the leaders suggested we write a journal to God. It became my diary to the Lord, and I have kept one periodically since I was 18 years old. To keep this memoir extremely personal, I will begin each chapter with the facts and my thoughts and then I will end the chapter conversing with God. My story begins with my marriage in 1995, so I will be looking back at past journals as I write each chapter.

People often refer to me as an inspiration because of my dogged determination in trying to get better. The Holy Spirit is often called the Inspirer because of His work in people's lives. More magnificent is His power in those who seek His help and guidance.

I pray that my story will inspire you; not by my desires and efforts, but by the saving and healing power of our Lord Jesus Christ.

Read on, and be inspired.

Chapter 1

A NEW BEGINNING

That is why a man leaves his father and mother and is united to his wife, and they become one flesh.

Genesis 2:24

No one believed I would ever do it. Me, live somewhere besides Louisville, Kentucky? It would never happen.

Falling in love can change all your plans. I felt like I had dated every bachelor in Louisville by the age of thirty-four, so when my friend Jennifer fixed me up with her friend from Little Rock, Arkansas, I did not immediately put him on the No list because he did not live in 'Luvall'.

I liked Drew immediately. He was funny, sarcastic, and he made me laugh. Southwest Airlines became our best buddy as we traveled back and forth to each others' homes. We were very much alike in our faithfulness to our respective hometowns. He made it very clear that he would never move, and as we became closer, I knew I was not just choosing a mate. I would be choosing a new city, far away from my family and friends.

I believed God was in our plans when a position with my pharmaceutical company opened in Little Rock. My boss in Louisville gave me a glowing recommendation, but after much discussion, we decided we were not going to let a job offer rush our future plans. When Drew did propose a few months later, a higher-level job with my company opened in Little Rock. They offered it to me immediately. Not only was my company moving me, they were promoting me as well!

Our upcoming nuptials called for many parties and get-togethers. It was the fairytale wedding I had always imagined. I slept very little in the months before the wedding. My mind was racing with hundreds of little details, and being a compulsive planner, I could not turn my brain off.

The wedding took place on March 18, 1995. Spring had come early that year. My friends and I ran wearing shorts earlier that morning. I was tickled that Wendy and Susan had made a large cardboard sign for me to wear on the front of my t-shirt. The sign read, *Bride getting married tonight. Last run as a single woman.* My bridesmaids congregated on my parents' patio while waiting their turn to have their make-up done. After months of cold, dreary winter, the sun felt wonderful as it warmed our faces and spilled over our shoulders.

Our wedding was at 7:30 PM in St. Agnes Catholic church, which had a long center aisle. I felt like Maria from the "Sound Of Music" as I walked down the aisle with my cathedral-length train. A string quartet played the songs Drew and I had selected, including my all-time favorite, *On Eagle's Wings,* with the lyrics taken from Psalm 91.

The chorus of that song was so beautiful! *"And He will raise you up on eagle's wings; bear you on the breath of dawn; make you to shine like the sun; and hold you in the palm of His hand."*

The reception was held in downtown Louisville at the crystal ballroom of the Brown Hotel. My father and I danced to *Edelweiss*, also from the "Sound of Music". My dad had taken me on a 'date' when I was six years old to see that classic when it first came out, and the music from the movie was very special to me.

Drew and I ended the evening by taking a horse-drawn carriage ride around downtown Louisville. Drew may have been a little bored, but it was my chance to say good-bye to the hometown that I loved. I thought I would be leaving forever.

We came home from our honeymoon to Little Rock, with all the dogwoods in bloom. We moved in with Drew's parents until our new home was ready. His mom, Bettye Jane, and I became fast friends. Not only did we both love home decorating, we were both closet smokers. We would commune every night after supper in the guest bathroom upstairs. Of course, Drew and his dad knew exactly what we were doing.

Our new home was in a small, gated community backing up to a golf course. Neither Drew nor I golfed, but I certainly had lots of new running trails. The home boasted a lovely lot, but we had to keep our bedroom blinds closed when it snowed, since all our neighbors used Hole Nine, just behind our house, for sledding, seemingly twenty-four hours a day, every day of the week.

The house itself had large rooms with hardwood floors, decorated in a 1980s contemporary motif. The decorator in me was offended. Bettye Jane and I spent an entire weekend scraping wallpaper in the kitchen. It took a whole week of evenings to scrape the powder room. When I looked at the pastel damask paper in our two-level entry hall, we decided to hire a professional painter. He was lovingly referred to as Duane, the painter, after a character in a 1980s sit-com, Murphy Brown. The men who worked on our house became a part of our family, so that year's family Christmas card was a picture of me, Drew, Duane, our carpenter, and the front door glass designer.

Pharmaceutical sales were more challenging for me in Little Rock. I grew up in a Louisville medical family, and was used to seeing doctors both professionally and socially. I also had a proven track record of sales, so my work team respected me. I did not know a single physician in Little Rock and had not yet proved myself to my work colleagues.

My new work team had not yet become like family, but I found a group to run with on weekends, thanks to my brother-in-law Dan. I even joined the Junior League of Little Rock. It was my way of getting to know this new community that was now my home. I was happy to realize that being married comes with an instant social life. All Drew's friends became my friends, too.

Most of that social life revolved around the Grande Maumelle Sailing Club. Drew's family had been sailors for many years. I became Drew's crew on his eighteen-foot sailing yacht, christened Shamrock. We also shared a thirty-foot yacht, called White Trash, with his brother Dan. Sailing was a way of life, just as tennis had always been for my family, but it really was not my cup of tea. I was never interested in water sports, but tried to keep an open mind. The people were so nice, after all!

After a year of marital bliss, I became pregnant. I was excited to see the changes in my body. Everyone said it was a boy, since I carried the baby straight out in my belly. Drew and I wanted to be surprised, so we closed our eyes during the ultrasound and asked not to be informed of the baby's gender.

Drew was called to another town three hours away for work just around my due date. Fortunately, my mom flew in from Louisville. After a nice dinner and visit at Bettye Jane's house, we went home for the night. I had just settled into bed, when I felt what seemed like a terrible menstrual cramp. *But that cannot be a cramp. I am pregnant!* When I had another one five minutes later, I went screaming upstairs. *Mom! I think I am in labor!*

Bettye Jane arrived about 10:00 PM. The three of us left for the hospital an hour later. Once I was settled, Bettye Jane walked with me up and down the corridors at the nurse's request. I was not sure why I was doing this; all I knew was that it hurt! I think we were attempting to bring on labor. *Oh good! More pain!* Drew drove all night to be there for the birth of our child. Would we have a healthy son or daughter? My labor began at 10:00 PM January 30th. Drew made it back to Little Rock an hour before the big arrival. Our son, Andrew, finally made his appearance at 6:00 PM on January 31st. *It's a boy!*

Our friends Les and Mina were our first visitors. My dad arrived from Louisville about 9:00 PM. My brother Andrew also flew in from South Carolina bearing Korbell Chardonnay to celebrate. I refused the offered pain medicine so I could partake in the celebration.

I referred to my brother Andrew as my favorite brother when I was younger. That is why I chose the name for my son. What a wonderful coincidence that it was also his father Drew's full name!

My whole family flew in for Andrew's baptism a few weeks later. He wore the same beautiful christening gown that we all wore as babies.

I have a few more spotty memories of Andrew's infancy before my accident. Unfortunately, the brain injury took most of them.

Dear Lord,

You have given me a brand new start in life. I am not a Varga anymore. I am now a Daugherty. Help me to bring the same confidence and compassion to my new life in Little Rock. I do not have the Varga family name to open doors for me anymore. I actually have to wait in doctors' offices now. Doors do not open for me in the pharmaceutical business here. I may know all the benefits and side effects of my drugs, and my competitors, but clients do not say, "Come on in!" to Mary Daugherty, like they did to Mary Varga. What a privileged life I had. What a silly thing to complain to You about!

Instead, You have given me a mate for life, a perfect son, terrific in-laws, a beautiful new home and a new job. Teach me to be a good door-opener. This is new territory for me.

Let me raise Andrew to be a faithful, loving, Catholic boy. Drew is not Catholic, but he is letting me lead the way with our son's faith life. So please lead me to make good and wise choices for him.

Thank You for this brand new beginning!

Chapter 2

<u>THE ACCIDENT</u>

In him was life, and that life was the light of all mankind. The light shines in the darkness, and the darkness has not overcome it.

John 1:4-5

When the brain suffers a trauma like the one I had, it does not record a memory , and that is actually a blessing in disguise. *Thank You God*! This part of my story comes from facts I was told over and over again by Drew or other family members. The feelings, however, I *do* remember.

It happened the day before my very first Mother's Day. I was looking forward to celebrating this special day for moms. Andrew was three months old already! We were expected at a cookout at Ben and Sherri Jo's house after the sailboat races. Drew was still at the sailing club. I stayed home to get myself and Andrew party-ready. When Drew finally arrived home, the party had already started. I left in a huff, taking

Andrew with me. Drew would have to take his own car after he showered.

Ben and Sherri Jo lived just over a mile away. I drove through the neighborhood just beyond our house. As I began to accelerate again after stopping at a stop sign, a teenage boy barreled down the intersecting hill and T-boned my car. He did not have a stop sign, so technically, it was my fault. Today, that same intersection is a four-way stop. I have seen pictures of our damaged automobiles. I had just begun accelerating, so the boy must have been moving at a pretty good clip to cause our cars to be as crushed as they were.

Fortunately, I had worn my seat belt, so I was not thrown from the car. My brain ricocheted back and forth inside my skull, held in place by the seatbelt. I had only minor scrapes, with no cuts or broken bones. Andrew still slept safely in his car seat.

My crockpot of piping-hot spinach dip that had been lying on the back seat floor was not so lucky. Dip went flying and splattering everywhere, including all over Andrew's car seat. Thankfully, he was still so tiny that I had placed his seat facing out the back window. Otherwise, the spinach dip would have burned his delicate skin instead of hitting the car seat.

The impact caused my body to go into a coma. An emergency room registered nurse (R.N.) named Bob happened to be standing in his friend's front yard and witnessed the whole accident. I asked Bob several years later if he had seen our cars collide. He told me he just saw my car land. Yikes! Apparently, the impact had launched my car airborne. No wonder it was scrunched!

Bob ran over to pull me out of the driver's seat. The teenager that hit me was in a sports utility vehicle. His car was crushed too, but he was walking around. Bob saw green stuff all over the back seat of my car and thought the baby had thrown up, but it was just the flying spinach dip. He gave me cardio-pulmonary resuscitation (CPR) and made sure I was breathing. Then he waited for the ambulance to arrive. The ladies in the neighborhood passed Andrew around during the wait.

An emergency room nurse just happened to be standing there when I had my accident? Many would call that a coincidence or freak luck, but I call it a God-intervention. I told that story many times over the years when explaining the particulars of the accident. Why did it take so many years for me to see God's hand there? Was it my trauma or my lack of faith? Perhaps it was the way the story was relayed to me by Drew or my family, since I was not conscious to experience the trauma.

Before I moved from Louisville, my brother Dan was my primary care physician. Apparently, I still had him listed in my wallet to call in case of emergency, so Dan got the call from the emergency medical services of Little Rock (E.M.S.) notifying him of my accident. My husband did not even know yet. Still, Dan was on the telephone giving E.M.S. my health and medical history. Drew only found out when he got to the party and Andrew and I were not there. He called our house and picked up a message from the hospital, saying that I was in the emergency room.

Within the next few hours, my entire family converged on Little Rock, hoping it was not the last time they would see their daughter/sister. The doctors said that if I made it through the night, I would probably survive. Some people have speculated that, as a runner, my excellent cardiovascular condition probably saved my life. Perhaps. I personally believe that God was not finished with me yet. He had a greater calling for my life than just to survive.

My accident was on May 10, 1997. I regained consciousness over the Fourth of July weekend. Coming out of the coma was a very gradual process. My first two weeks were spent in critical care on a ventilator. When I was able to breathe on my own, I was moved to a step-down unit with four other patients. My eyes were open most of the day, but in spite of appearances, no one was home.

What a journey the next few months would be! My dad tells me that while I was in the step-down unit, my legs jerked around wildly in my hospital bed. I told him perhaps I was dreaming I was running a race. I now know that is what happens when brain pathways are disconnected. My brain did not understand that lying down called for stillness.

The nurses did not want to strap me in my bed, so for my own safety, they put my mattress on the floor. That way I wouldn't have far to fall if my thrashing around brought me to the edge of the bed.

According to Dad, the first words out of my coma were not very gentle. The night nurse was checking my vital signs. I sat straight up in my bed and said, "Who the hell are you?" What a grand entrance into the world of conscious living!

My parents rented an apartment in Little Rock while I was in the hospital. They wanted to be able to accommodate family and friends when they flew down to see me. Mom stayed during the week, and Dad drove down every weekend, after his last patient left on Friday.

My parents said they rarely saw Drew at the hospital. I suppose he came at night after his work day was finished. I do remember him visiting one night with our baby, Andrew. In my memory, it was dark in the room, with light only from the hall. Just how late was it?

My first memory is of waking up in a bedroom with my mother sitting at my side in a chair, reading. I asked where I was. When she told me I was in a hospital, my first question was, "Where's Dad?" I figured that if it was a hospital, Dad could not be far away. No questions about Drew or Andrew. Did I even remember them at that point?

Once fully aware of my surroundings, I became keenly aware of my immobility. I did not even know how to use a walker yet. At first, I felt trapped in the bed. Then I discovered scooting on my bottom was an efficient way to move my body around. The social side of me wanted to know what was going on. So I would scoot out to the nurses' station and pull myself up to the counter. I had worked in hospitals for so many years; this seemed the logical place to find out what was happening. Then I would scoot down the hallway just for the exercise of it.

When I got tired, I would scoot back to my room. I always had the television on. Princess Diana had recently died in a terrible car accident. Her life was being remembered and her passing mourned all over the world. She was so young! That could easily have been me. At this point, I was so traumatized by my inability to walk that Princess Diana's death was just news on the television. This may also have been the first sign of my nearly all-consuming self-centeredness. Would I ever be able to be happy or sad for anyone else again, or were my physical limitations going to eat me alive?

Hi Lord!

You know what happened to me. You know how I am suffering! I did not have a rosary in my hospital room, so I prayed the rosary on my fingers last night. You think Mary heard me? Did You? I really need to know You are with me right now. My life has fallen apart. Thank You for giving me such a caring, supportive family, though. This has been such a tragic shock to all of them. I feel such comfort in their love for me. Mom and Dad will do whatever is possible to bring me happiness again. Poor Drew. Please comfort him too. I think he must be grieving the death of the wife he fell in love with. He does not seem to even recognize this handicapped lady who looks just like her.

There are so many hurting people who do not have family and friends, or the financial means to help them get better. Even in this tragedy, You have truly blessed me.

Chapter 3

ENTERING THE TUNNEL

In my distress I called to the Lord; I cried to my God for help. From his temple he heard my voice; my cry came before him, into his ears.

Psalm 18:6

When I first began having rational thoughts after my coma, the first ones that I cried out to were my parents, not God. They were the ones who gave me immediate comfort in times of trouble. I'm sure that's why God placed them there. I called out to Him when I was lying in bed at night. My prayers were not specific requests, but rather the routine, methodical prayers I had learned as a child.

I didn't have a rosary, so I used my fingers to count off ten *Hail Marys* and one *Our Father*. It was not an open dialog with God, but my prayers were uttered with such great fervor that He must surely have heard me. In my heart and soul I was pleading with the Almighty just as King David did in the book of Psalms.

I was distressed, confused and terrified. My life had just changed on a dime. Mom, Dad and God were the three I innately turned to for comfort. *Please let me wake up and realize this was just a nightmare, Lord!*

I had no balance; my coordination was shot. My extremely monotone voice made one lose interest in talking to me, even if one could understand me. Aside from those setbacks, I looked and felt fine.

I am of course, being facetious there. Looking good had always been important to me, but not at the expense of my mobility and coordination. I looked crippled. I was crippled! Life was not at all happy, for me or anyone around me. Yet the ministrations of caring family and friends continued.

Mom and Dad were my constants. My sister Julie has often teased me about her first visit to see me in the hospital. Every time she left the room, she would reintroduce herself when she returned. It seems my memory—especially my short-term memory—was nonexistent when I first came out of my coma. I could not remember Julie or who she was whenever she left my immediate presence. I have been told of other friends and family who came to see me as well, but unfortunately, those memories did not remain in my injured brain.

My sister-in-law, Missy, just back from her honeymoon with my brother Paul, flew down to stay with me the last two weeks in the hospital. Missy has joked about eating meals with me in a patient dining room. I would bring a fork full of food to my mouth and it would dribble down the front of my top. She always had to tell me, "Lean forward, Mary. Lean forward." So I credit Missy with teaching me how to eat again. Missy stayed on to get me settled back at home, making sure that all living spaces were accessible.

Michele, milkshakes and my potty mouth

During my hospital stay, I invented an imaginary friend named Michele. According to my family, Michele and I were always going out to lunch, shopping or gabbing on the telephone. One day, my mother commented on the new drawings I had attached to the bulletin board in my hospital room. They were obviously done by a child. Mom asked me who they were from. I shrugged, saying "It must have been Michele's kids." I think that was the first of many efforts I have made over the years since to feel connected to people and to pretend I have a normal life.

I have been told that next to the bulletin board in my hospital room there was a large banner displaying all the signatures and remarks from the medical staff at Jewish Hospital in Louisville. I had worked at Jewish Hospital in physician/hospital marketing for years before I jumped over to the pharmaceutical industry. My boss and good friend, Carole, placed the banner in the doctors' lounge for a few days before coming down to see me in Little Rock. It upsets me that no one thought to bring the banner home from the hospital, since I have no memory of that, either.

I have always prided myself on being small and fit. I was not blessed with a high metabolism, but with a great desire to stay slim. Running and counting calories had been my way to achieve a petite frame. Doughnuts, candy bars or pies never touched my lips. Milkshakes were completely forbidden...until I had my brain injury. Since I was allowed to leave the hospital on occasion, Purple Cow became a routine stop for large, chocolate milk shakes. I would daydream about them. Eating had become a way of bringing enjoyment into my life again.

My weight had gotten down to ninety-five pounds while I was in the coma, on tube feedings, so I needed to gain some weight. Then I gained so much that none of my clothes fit! I immediately went into diet mode, but could not get the weight off. Then I discovered that the hospital was not giving me the thyroid medication I had been taking since age twenty. Once I started it again, within a few months I was down to a normal weight for my size.

Another notable characteristic of my recovering brain, that has been the topic of many humorous family dinners, was my extremely profane language. Dad has often said that I used language that would make a sailor blush. In the early stages of recovery, a brain injury survivor can be very aggressive and impulsive. No one was exempt from my tyranny—doctors, nurses, family or friends. My favorite word seemed to be the F-word.

Family had been alerted to my impulsiveness before they visited. When my 'favorite brother' Andrew came to see me, he thought our close relationship would exonerate him from my behavior. He walked into the room saying, "Hey Mare!" I replied, "F...you Andrew! F...you!" I have no memory of the visit. Does that exonerate me?

My brother Dan tried to stop my cursing by getting me to focus on the photo album of family and friends they had placed in my room. He kept asking me to identify different faces in the pictures. "Who is this girl in the blue shirt? Is that Stephanie?" The ploy worked...temporarily.

A few years after my accident, Drew arranged for me to be a volunteer on the same brain injury unit where I had been a patient. Seeing hospital staff that had been there during my stay usually prompted me to reassure the person, "Don't worry. I am not mean anymore." One of the therapists told me that they celebrate when they see patients behaving as I did, because that means the brain is recovering.

The Varga family members have always been very 'take charge' individuals, especially my dad. My recovery was no exception. My only memory of Drew during this time was his exasperation with my behavior. How horrible it must have been to see the woman he loved behave in such a fashion. He refused to let me come back to Louisville for intensive therapy, saying that he wanted his wife with him. He did agree to two weeks of private home therapy that my father had arranged in Louisville.

After driving back to Louisville with Mom and Dad, I spent three hours each day with a physical therapist, an occupational therapist and a speech therapist. I felt like I was back in school again, and could not wait for them to leave.

Sleeping became my means of escape. I secretly wished that I would wake up normal and realize it had all been a bad dream. In the meantime, I was becoming something I never wanted to be—an object of pity! Oh please God! Let me wake up from this nightmare.

My potty mouth had gone away by this time. Now I wanted my disabilities to go away too. Running and being active were a big part of my life. What was I supposed to do now? I could not walk without a walker. I had this goofy, raspy voice that no one could understand. I could no longer drive or work. What had my life become?

Dear Lord,

This is a nightmare. Besides my family ,everything that I identified with in this life has been taken away from me. I suppose I am thankful You spared my life. I am not very thankful for it right now. I am holding on to the belief that You will make something good from this tragedy.

Thank You for all of my Varga family. They have truly loved me, warts and all. I cannot say the same thing about my in-laws, though. I just feel that I have disappointed them terribly. Thank You also for all the notes, books, and words of encouragement from my friends in Louisville. I guess I did something right during my first 35 years.

Chapter 4

Learning to be Disabled

Come to me, all you who are weary and burdened, and I will give you rest. Take my yoke upon you and learn from me, for I am gentle and humble in heart, and you will find rest for your souls.

Matthew11:28-29

My first week home from the hospital, my mother-in-law brought me a velvet lounging robe. *Are you kidding? What am I supposed to do with this?* It was an attractive garment meant to make someone feel pretty during their infirmity. Maybe Bettye Jane thought I was going to get over this like a virus. Is this how people saw me now...as an invalid to be put on a shelf with a pretty robe?

Since I was clearly not mobile enough to care for six-month-old Andrew, Drew hired a nanny to stay with him during the day. Her name was Torsha. She also cleaned the house, took me to the grocery and to the athletic club. I suppose personal assistant was also part of her job description. I could no longer drive, but taking me anywhere required more than just a driver's license and an automobile. Torsha had to get my walker into and out of the car. It had to be positioned at just the right angle by my door, or I might lose my balance. She had to go into the grocery store with me too, because at 5'2", I could not reach items on the higher shelves.

I recall one horrific trip to Kroger. For many months after my brain injury, I had little control over my bladder muscles. We were in the cereal aisle and I could not hold it any longer, so I peed right there under the Captain Crunch. Fortunately, there was an employee nearby to clean up my spill. I was very ashamed and humiliated. Is this how Jesus felt as he carried the cross? Was it any comfort to know that He freely chose it? I did not choose to lose control of my bladder. Knowing that my head trauma had provoked it was no comfort. I felt out of control of my own body.

Torsha took me home to change my gym shorts before we headed to the Little Rock Athletic Club. I went there several days each week to do a cardio workout and lift weights. I discovered that people treat handicapped individuals very cautiously. I had poor balance, but I would not break if you touched me!

Eventually, those same folks would get a kick out of me. They seemed surprised that I was so strong and flexible, and knew my way around the gym so well. I would walk around the running track while Torsha wheeled my walker behind me. I was painfully slow and awkward. My legs still wanted to run, but I could not allow them to because of my balance.

It was on one of these walking jaunts that my friend Nancy saw me for the first time. It was hard not to notice me, as clumsy as I appeared. Nancy had an immediate vision of doctors discussing my condition and how to make it better. We did not meet that day; instead she called Drew explaining her vision and asked if she could come over. Drew was very intrigued and hopeful. After meeting Nancy with Drew, we decided to go to lunch on our own to get to know each other better.

Nancy and I had lunch before coming back to my house to talk. I was explaining the different pharmaceutical drugs I sold and how stiff the competition was. Nancy later told me that Drew had given her the impression that I did not understand much of what I said. She was surprised and delighted to see how intelligent I was. It was Nancy who first urged me to write my story. Eighteen years later, she was glad I finally got around to it.

Drew did everything he could to help me get better, but unknowingly left me humiliated on many occasions. He used to take me out with friends in inappropriate clothes and without any make-up. I know he was just trying to make my life easier. He had me convinced I looked just as good without make-up. Who was he kidding? I knew I at least needed the help of a mascara wand.

I began to be obsessed with trying to walk again. I was totally consumed with performing the exercises the physical therapists had given me. I wanted so much to have my life back again! Walking through the first floor of our house, including three trips around the dining room table without a walker, was my own self-subscribed daily exercise program. I figured it would become easier if I kept practicing. It did not, yet I had become addicted to exercise. Between the daily gym visit and my home program, I was spent every day.

In Hebrews 12:12-13, God says, T*herefore, strengthen your feeble arms and weak knees. Make level paths for your feet, so that the lame may not be disabled, but rather healed.* When I read these words, I thought Jesus wanted me to keep pushing myself. Eighteen years later, I still believe He does. Now I understand that He gave us the skilled eyes of physical therapists to correct our wrong movements and show us the right way. He then gives us patience and hope until life turns around.

One truth I learned in my new life as a disabled person is that people usually do not ask for my opinion. Speaking was a real challenge with my new brain-injured voice. It was hard to understand and made me sound stupid. I am not just imagining things either! Sales clerks would always talk to the friend with me, rather than with me, when I was making a purchase. Usually, I let it go, but on one particularly frustrating day, I quipped, *I am the one with the credit card! Perhaps you should talk to me.* I immediately felt bad. It was not the poor clerk's fault that she could not understand me.

I could not seem to get it through my thick skull that I was now disabled. I still looked the same, but when I opened my mouth to talk, people knew I was different. Even if I was sitting down with no walker beside me, my raspy voice would give me away. If you guess I'm embarrassed by my handicaps, that would be a correct assumption. I am not the best conversationalist in the world. I do not get out much. My sister Julie, in trying to help me, told me that people like to talk about themselves, *so ask a lot of questions*! Unfortunately, my voice was very soft, and in large gatherings when conversing required volume, I felt awkward. It can be difficult to ask questions when no one can hear you. So I usually stood there smiling, and feeling out-of-place. Now, I generally shy away from large groups. When the volume goes up, I do best to steer clear.

In order to maintain my balance, I have to consciously think about how my body is moving. It is challenging to walk and talk at the same time. If someone asks me to take a walk and talk about some issue, I have to decline. I have to sit to give my attention to anything other than staying upright. Multitasking is no longer in my vocabulary.

The hardships I lived with because of my balance and voice were endless. How I managed them, though, made the difference between being a kind Christian lady or a frustrated handicapped lady. We are told in Philippians 2:14-15, *Do everything without grumbling or arguing, so that you may become blameless and pure, children of God without fault in a warped and crooked generation. Then you will shine among them like stars in the sky.*

I can almost hear my family snickering right now. They have certainly heard their share of grumbling and complaining in the last eighteen years. They especially do not like to hear me complain because they love me, and there is usually nothing they can do to remedy the problem. It makes them feel powerless.

I believe complaining is a sin against God as well. *Nothing is impossible for God...* except for my circumstance. That thought shows a complete lack of trust in God's power in our lives.

Dear Lord,

What can I possibly say to redeem myself? I am just like the Israelites with all my murmuring and complaining. You know the hardships I deal with everyday. Please let me use some of that wonderful strength You gave me to hold my tongue. No one wants to hear about my problems, even if they love me. It just makes them feel inadequate to do anything to help me.

I ask for a medical breakthrough to heal my infirmities. I ask for the patience to wait for it expectantly.

You have been such a compassionate and loving Father through this whole ordeal. I ask that You let me be a blessing to all those who have worked so hard for me. Hang in there with me, Jesus. I cannot do this alone.

Chapter 5

ANOTHER PUNCH IN THE GUT

In this world *you will have trouble. But take heart! I have overcome the world.*

John 16:33

Life in Little Rock went on as usual after my accident. I had grown accustomed to not having balance or coordination. Being different from everybody else was becoming a way of life.

Oddly enough, I had long dreamed of being unique and different from everyone else. Being one of six children can give you that dream. All I can say is, *be careful what you pray for!* Now I am seen as different because of my disabilities rather than because of my noble qualities. *I am still Mary in here!*

Unfortunately, I now came packaged as a handicapped lady. Sometimes I was even the cute little handicapped lady. Others could not see beyond that package. All my former self-descriptions seemed to disappear: runner, drug rep, Drew's wife, Andrew's mom. It was as if I had no identification outside of my disabilities.

Drew became different with me then, too. He was no longer my friend and lover. He was my caregiver. He was an excellent caregiver, but I wanted my husband back. He shared nothing with me. Drew used to refer to the person I was before the accident as the *Old Mary*. Now I had become the *New Mary*. Up to this point I had believed that *new* was better than *old*. Drew had given me a new spin on things.

My life as Andrew's mother was grossly different. I could no longer hold him, feed him, change or dress him. That is what mothers do; I could do none of it. When he got older, I taught him how to pray. But all those precious early moments were already lost. Andrew did not seem to know what my role was. He showed very little respect for me. Who was this lady who lived with his dad and the babysitter?

About three years after my accident, my parents brought Andrew and me back to Louisville for what they lovingly referred to as Mommy Camp. My dad drove to Little Rock and brought us back to Louisville for two weeks of intensive training. The goal was to teach me how to be a mom. Since Andrew was just three months old when I had my brain injury, I missed most of his early childhood recovering. If I had ever learned, I subsequently forgot how to be a mom.

During Mommy Camp, I fed him, dressed him, bathed him and played with him all day. I was afraid I would gain weight not working out for two weeks, but I found that keeping up with a three-year-old is quite the calorie burner. I even had him doing sit-ups with me. By the time "camp" was over, he was a different little boy. He would talk to me, play with me, behave for me, and most importantly, WAIT for me.

When we returned to Little Rock, his behavior continued. I could not keep him away from me. But after about three weeks, he resumed shouting at me, ignoring me and not doing what I asked him. I called my parents, crying for a Mommy Camp #2. But my separation from Drew occurred before it could happen.

On November 9, 2000, Drew came home unexpectedly in the middle of the day. He said he was home to meet my father. "Dad's coming? Why did you not tell me?" I was so excited!

Then Drew told me Dad was coming to take me home because he was divorcing me. I just stared at him. I could not catch my breath. I had always wondered what it would be like to receive such horrible news. I just stared! I was stunned!

I felt as if my luck had just run out. Who would want to live with a handicapped woman, pretty or not; nice or not? In my mind, I was getting what I had coming to me. Drew tried to make me feel better by inviting his mother, Bettye Jane, over to the house. We were such good friends! He even allowed us to smoke in the house, although smoking inside was never allowed.

This was the first time I really regretted not being able to cry. I have not cried in eighteen years. The brain pathway that connects emotions with tears has been severed. I produce tears when I peel an onion, but not when something makes me sad. Bettye Jane was crying, and I wanted to also! I thought it would make me feel better, but instead, I just stared as I watched the rest of my life fall apart.

I was so relieved when my dad arrived. He was surprised that I knew already. He had asked Drew to wait until he was there for support. Apparently, Drew had flown to Louisville two days before, asking my dad to meet him at the airport, and that is where he dropped the news of the divorce. So my entire family knew my heart-breaking news days before I did! Boy, did I feel like the poor little handicapped lady now.

Dad thought I would take a day or two to pack, but I just wanted to get out of there as quickly as I could. I went from drawer to drawer to closet throwing things in large trash bags. Drew's sister-in-law was keeping Andrew and was prepared to bring him back at a moment's notice. Since his behavior had returned to the pre-Mommy Camp days, I was unsure of how he would react to the news that I was leaving. Out of fear that he would not even care, I chose not to see him. At that point, I was just putting one foot in front of the other.

Since my accident, moving around had been a constant challenge. *Can I get the walker in there? Do I have to maneuver any steps? Is the space too tight?* Even as my heart was breaking, those were immediate concerns that needed to be addressed. At that point in my recovery, it was very difficult to talk or react to anything while I was in the process of walking, and walking was definitely a process! *Please let this become second nature for me, Lord!*

As is typical for my dad, we had a pre-dawn departure. We stopped in front of the house so I could have one last look back. Drew was waving from the front office window. I could not stop staring at the beautiful cut-glass front doors I had designed. I turned to Dad, "Mind if I smoke?"

The eight-hour drive back to Louisville was uneventful. Dad let me speak first to the current crisis. I was speculating on whether the Catholic Church would approve of the divorce. "Should I get a legal separation instead?" Dad responded, "Just divorce him and be done with it".

We arrived home to Mom's beef stew and biscuits. I was dreading a pity party. "*I am so sorry!*" was the only thing Mom said...that night. After dinner, family members started filing in one-by-one. They were there to welcome me home. I was deeply moved. Although my family is usually a loud and boisterous group, no one quite knew what to say. "Hey Mare! So great to have you back!"

My sister Julie helped me unpack and organize my clothes. Little did she know her work wardrobe was about to expand. We were both the same size and both in the pharmaceutical business. No telling what Arkansas fashion treasures she would find! I certainly would not be wearing business attire any time soon.

Psalm 34:18 tells us, *The LORD is close to the brokenhearted and saves those who are crushed in spirit.* I felt Jesus holding me in His arms that night as my family hugged me and welcomed me back. It was not a pity party at all, but a true show of love and support for their sister who had come home.

When I settled into my bedroom that night, I picked up my book, *God Calling,* and read what God had to say about this day. The excerpt for November 10 was entitled *New Forces.* This is how it started: "Remember that life's difficulties and troubles are not intended to arrest your progress, but to increase your speed. You must call new forces, new powers into action." Was God speaking to me personally? It surely felt like it. Better yet, it sounded like a challenge to me! It gave me great peace to know He was controlling this situation.

Dear Lord,

What am I supposed to do now? I have truly lost everything. No! I have not! Sorry Jesus…just being melodramatic. Do I even know how to think for myself anymore? My behavior just seems to be a reflection of other people's reactions to me. You know I have always thought my family's opinion on things was gold. Thank You that they are reflecting silent composure to me now. I do not know how I would react if they were being emotional. My daily life is changing dramatically. Thank You that I do not feel a gaping hole because Drew is gone. He checked out emotionally a long time ago. Watch over him and Andrew tonight.

Thank You for giving me a family to stand with me, so that the abandonment does not feel so awful. Drew and I live in different states now. No danger of running in to him. Thank You for the numbness I feel about everything tonight. Is this how You are protecting me from this day?

Your words in 'God Calling' were so comforting tonight. Thank You for the 'New Forces' that You will call into play here in Louisville.

Chapter 6

<u>BACK ON BUNKER HILL</u>

For I know the plans I have for you, declares the LORD, plans for welfare and not for evil, to give you a future and a hope.

Jeremiah 29:11

I woke the next morning greatly relieved to be back in the home I grew up in. My appetite had left me, but I surely did want coffee and a cigarette. What was happening in the news? I do not remember now, and I did not care then. I was still so very numb from what had happened.

I just wanted to see my mother's face and hear her lovely sarcasm. I felt like a little girl again, just trying to drink in all the familiar sights and sounds of home, where people loved me. We had stayed up late sampling rich after-dinner drinks. Mom would not be up for hours.

My body's time clock had recently changed to wake me early in the morning. I can remember calling my dad from Little Rock at 5:30 AM because I knew he was already up. Now I was waking up to the sound of him unloading the dishwasher right outside my door. My father's early morning dish-clanging used to drive Drew nuts when we would visit Louisville. Now, it was music to my ears, as well as my alarm clock.

Dad would bring my coffee mug out to the sunroom where we would read the newspaper and watch the NBC morning news. Then, while he did the morning crossword puzzle, I would read from Robert Schuller's daily devotional, *Hours of Power*. I wanted so much to know what God was trying to teach me.

I am still trying to discover God's heart. I have the Christian books, CDs, and DVDs to testify to my constant hunger to know God's will. Sometimes I feel as though I am reading a self-help book. Is that not what all Christian reading (including the Bible) is, though? We are glorifying   God   while   we   help   ourselves.

Friends, Rehab and Divorce Proceedings

The thought of explaining my presence in Louisville kept me from calling any friends the first week I was home. I was not ready to discuss any of the details of being jilted. A week after I arrived, though, my friend Norma called. Drew had called her from Little Rock to tell her what happened, and Norma told me she could not wait any longer for me to call. She came over a few minutes later.

I was so happy to see Norma! We had been friends since college. She and her husband Chas had come to see us once in Little Rock. Just like my family, Norma just told me how sorry she was and how excited she was to have me back home. She *did* tell me how impressed she was that Drew had called to prepare her before seeing me. I was impressed, too. It was time to stop hiding.

My former pharmaceutical sales team stopped over one afternoon. They expressed their sorrow, but were able to make me laugh as they had before. Word seemed to travel fast that I was back in Louisville. I had many visitors, most of whom had not even seen me since my brain injury. Friends seemed confused as to which trauma to offer their condolences on...my disabilities or my divorce.

Words cannot describe how comforting it was to be with my mother during this time. Her child was hurt. She did everything she could to make the heartache more bearable. Just like when I was sick as a child, that meant lots of Diet Cokes, ice cream and movies.

About ten days after my return, the mailman delivered the official document requiring my signature, stating that Drew was filing for divorce. A friend of mine and Drew's had given my dad the name of an attorney with one of the top law firms in Little Rock. It was time to give him a call.

Dad also called a colleague at a local hospital to register me for three weeks of intensive inpatient rehabilitation. It was the same hospital where I had worked for five years after college. Again, I felt like I was going home. I was more than happy to work on improving my balance and gait, since I *hated* being disabled. I felt like I had gone back in time, walking the same hallways that used to be my work home. Every day I passed employees who still remembered me from twenty years ago. I made a point of visiting the auditorium where I had taught aerobic dance classes for employees for many years. I had to laugh as I wheeled my walker across the carpet. God willing, maybe someday!

While I was in the hospital, my therapy sessions frequently included other patients. These patients were usually twenty to thirty years older than me, recuperating from either a stroke, or hip or knee replacement. My enjoyment and comfort level with these patients would serve me well in the new career I would eventually launch.

My parents came to the hospital to visit me one night. I could tell they had something unpleasant to tell me, because they kept fidgeting! Dad started. "Drew is suing for sole custody of Andrew, claiming you are not mentally competent." I was stunned. This damned brain injury had already taken my mobility. Now my husband was using it to try to take my son.

Dad had already conferred with my physicians. They were prepared to give me intelligence tests and sign any statements necessary to confirm my mental competency. If I did not agree to Drew's sole custody of Andrew, it would require my appearance in court. My attorney thought that would definitely work in my favor, but did not want me to go through the anguish and the cost of a court appearance. He would put ample visitation into the divorce settlement to ensure I saw Andrew throughout the year. So I gave up custodial rights to Andrew. I have lived to regret that decision numerous times in the last eighteen years.

I had often teased that Drew thought I was retarded since my brain injury. Sometimes I even used that belief to my advantage. When Drew had his sailing buddies over, I would excuse myself to go play solitaire on the computer because I was so incredibly bored with all the sailing jargon. I knew that Drew believed it was my brain injury that caused me to be so rude. Were my solitaire games coming back to haunt me now?

It was a long, arduous process to unravel a lifetime commitment. My father acted as my Power of Attorney since it was so challenging for my attorney or anyone else to understand my brain-injured voice. Dad's main concern was for my financial future. After much back and forth, our attorneys arrived at a divorce settlement on which both Drew and I could agree. I had a settlement amount in my mind that I would be satisfied with. Our attorneys came up with a somewhat larger sum, so I surprised Drew with a personal check for the difference between the two amounts. I saw it as one final act of kindness as we severed our life together.

Dear Lord,

Please be my guide as I start this life all over again. In some ways, though, I feel like I never left Louisville. Thank You for giving me such a loving, stable family...especially Dad. What would I do without him? He has really taken the sting out of this abandonment by Drew.

I do not like feeling like a victim. Guess that is what I am right now, though. I still cannot fathom Drew's behavior. Did he really just expect me to say okay to him taking Andrew from me? He is not the man I thought he was. We prayed together every night for a few months. Was that just a show to him? How does he feel about all of this? Does he even care that he is ripping my heart out? I am so angry at him, but I still love him. How is that even possible?

You know I have always compared every man I met to Dad. Is that why I stayed single for so long? I suppose he will become the man in my life again, now that Drew is gone. Will any man ever want me again? I really do not care right now. I just want to have my balance back. Bet I could find a man then.

I just reread what I wrote to You. Just like the Israelites, I was grumbling and complaining. At the same time, I am so eternally grateful You have given me family and friends to make the unthinkable almost bearable.

Thank You also for faith that makes me believe that I will rise above this.

Chapter 7

Trying to Fix It

For physical training is of some value, but godliness has value for all things, holding promise for both the present life and the life to come.

1 Timothy 4:8

Now with my marriage dissolved and my son taken away, the only dream that kept me moving forward was my quest to walk again. I thanked God every day that I came from a medical family, believing that my dad or brothers would certainly hear about any new medical breakthroughs before the general public. This brings me comfort now after I have tried and failed at every therapy and treatment I have attempted.

As a former distance runner, I was completely hooked on the daily adrenalin rush you receive when your heart and lungs have been pushed beyond their usual capacity. Running was my time to reflect on upcoming or past events and milestones. It was also the time to make grocery lists, calculate the calories I was burning, and pray.

I immediately discovered that long walks with a walker accomplished the same thing. On one particularly refreshing Saturday morning, I walked from my parents' house up to Bardstown Road, and back. That was a jaunt of 1.8 miles that I had clocked many times as a runner. Depending on my speed, it took me fifteen to eighteen minutes to run that course. The same distance took me two hours and fifteen minutes using a walker. Suffice it to say, I had plenty of time to reflect.

Therapy: practice, practice, practice

I have requested numerous rounds of physical therapy in the last eighteen years. Every time, I begin with a new resolve to improve my balance and walking gait. I leave the first few sessions hopeful and praising my therapist.

My mission has always been to get off of that blamed walker. It makes me look and feel so crippled! People do not look at me. The first thing they see is the walker. How did I look at people on walkers before my accident? I wondered what happened to them, but I always thought it was probably a temporary issue. My imbalance is not. Unless or until there is a medical breakthrough, my balance will not improve significantly. I am able to make my muscles stronger and more toned, but the imbalance comes from an injured brain. I have trained my body to move correctly; that is what therapy is all about. However, my new normal is to lose my balance whenever challenged. There are fingerprints all over my walls, tables and counters to prove that point.

The experts said that the brain never stops recuperating, but most of that recovery was in the first eighteen months after the brain injury. Progress was slow after that.

I had to learn how to use a walker, which was fairly quick and painless. It had this handy bag on the front to store my purse and other essentials. I could really move quickly with a walker, until I ran up against steps or curbs. I was eventually able to conquer curbs to the point where they just slowed me down a bit.

My battle with stairs continued, though. Without a hand rail or someone to hang on to, my only safe option was to sit down and move down one step at a time. Talk about looking crippled!

After a few years, I graduated to a forearm crutch for walking. It was just like the one my grandfather, Pawpaw, had used because he had a stroke that paralyzed his right side. Pawpaw had to move slowly. Of course, I did not want to do that. I fell enough times to realize my balance would no longer allow me to move quickly, so I began to practice and practice and practice.

Years later, with a lot of physical therapy and practice, I started walking with a cane. It required no effort to get the cane in the car or through the doorway. It was as close to normal as I thought I would ever get. I still kept my walker nearby for trips that required speed or extra stability. This time, however, I procured a walker with wheels. Now I could walk at a normal pace with everyone else! My body was learning to balance!

One day, Jesus gave me the courage to walk across the entire room with no apparatus or wall to help me. I did it! I was so excited I *wanted* to practice that one again. I was walking with no assistance. *Thank You Jesus!*

I was still living with Mom and Dad at the time. I did not say anything to my family. Did they not notice? I was confused. The next afternoon, Dad looked at me saying, "Getting pretty cocky, aren't you?" He knew it was not a miracle, but sheer guts that allowed me to walk. He strongly encouraged me to still use the cane when I went out anywhere. I followed Dad's advice...for a while.

The first place I tried to walk without the cane was my health club, my home away from home. Everyone noticed and congratulated me. That is when I realized that it was still very difficult for me to balance while looking someone in the eye. So I did not look people in the eye unless seated. Turning to answer a question was out of the question. Walking without assistance made me feel normal, but I certainly did not look that way. I looked very unsteady.

Dena was my physical therapist at my health club. She once referred to me as the Energizer Bunny. She would see me walk along, fall down, get right back up, and keep going. Just like the bunny in the commercial, I would "take a licking and keep on ticking."

I find it challenging and sometimes humorous to attempt walking while carrying multiple packages, even if they're not heavy. It would be much easier to use two hands, but I need one hand to hold my cane. I will usually drop something, but picking it up requires balance. After several drops and pick-ups, I sometimes sit on the floor and laugh. *I'm glad nobody is watching!* I've had shoes slip off and purses that strangled me, which leads to the next thing I tried to *fix*.

Footwear and Purses

With a petite 5 foot 2 inch frame, I boasted a large closet of two- to three-inch heels in order to be fashionable and not towered over. They all had to be given away when I had my brain injury. No one in my family wore a size seven. When my therapist determined I had a leg-length discrepancy, they custom-made a heel-lift to go in my left shoe. That meant saying good-bye to all of my sling-back sandals.

Once, when I was pregnant with Andrew, I remember running through a hospital parking lot with three-inch heels, carrying a satchel full of drug samples trying to escape the cold. I could not button my coat, since my belly was too big. Post-pregnancy and post-brain injury, my coat buttoned easily. Running and heels were both a thing of the past, though. Now I just take it slowly and shiver.

Buying shoes became complicated. They not only had to fit my right foot, but my left, heel-lifted foot as well. No more going in and just grabbing a size seven. I had to bring them home and walk in them for several hours to make sure I could balance without my toes being pinched. Of course, they had to be flat, with no heel at all.

Carrying purses was another dilemma. Every woman knows the importance of having a fashionable bag to carry all their stuff in. It was part of the total look. Most ladies have also experienced neck or shoulder pain as a result of lugging a too-heavy purse on their shoulder. Did your purse ever cause you to lose your balance, though? This was an ongoing struggle for me, so I had to lose some of my stuff.

I tried shoulder bags, cross-bodies, clutches, backpacks and fanny packs. Backpacks were the best for keeping my posture in line, but they were a real hassle to get into! Cross-bodies got stuck in my hood. Shoulder bags fell off my shoulder, and the sudden weight shift would challenge anyone's balance. Clutches were cumbersome, and fanny packs gave the appearance of a large tumor on your hip. What was a girl to do? I had to make sure any purse I carried was light so it would not throw my balance off. No heavy leather bags for me!

I carried my cell phone in my sports bra. I will admit that it looked odd when I reached down my top to answer a call or text. It was handy, though. My sister-in-law, Tracy, introduced me to the SPIBelt, the Small Personal Items Belt. It was just one inch thick, expandable, and attached around the waist, so all I could carry was keys, a brush and cash.

Posture Control

At five feet two inches tall, I had always tried to walk and sit with perfect posture, in an effort to appear taller. My lack of balance since my brain injury caused me to lean forward to protect my body. I was constantly telling myself to hold my shoulders back, lift my chest, elevate my rib cage, and a dozen other mental cues I used to keep my torso up.

Holding my body in the proper alignment became an obsession for me. I cringed when I saw pictures of myself after my brain injury. I may have had a pretty smile, but I was always leaning. I hated it! I did not look normal.

As I write this, I am at the computer wearing a heavy backpack to keep my shoulders back, a neck brace to keep my head from leaning forward and sitting on a balance ball to keep my core muscles strong. I have the best computer posture in town. Would you agree this is a little obsessive? It surely helps when you are writing a book, though.

My Raspy Voice

What can I say about my voice? It is better than it was eighteen years ago. At first it was very monotone and nearly impossible to understand. Mom could only understand me if she was sitting in the room with me; then she could read my lips.

We used to pray the rosary out loud in the afternoons. Mom would recite the first part of the *Hail Mary* and I would recite the last part. Then we would both pray the *Our Father.* I read my prayers out loud every morning too. It helped me with my enunciation of words. Slowly, my voice began to have inflection again.

Andrew and I prayed the rosary out loud one afternoon when it appeared that car trouble was going to cause him to miss a sailboat regatta with his dad in Indiana. We were praying the third decade of the rosary when my phone rang. Drew had found alternate transportation and was on his way. Andrew was convinced it was our prayer. He was so elated that he could not sit still. I convinced him, though, to finish our rosary in thanksgiving for our answered prayer.

How many times did I pray for God to cure my funky voice? It did become more understandable over the years. It was really frustrating to have people not understand me. Sometimes they would pretend like they did, but that was even more frustrating. I think I would rather have heard them say, "Huh?"

Sometimes I felt as if I needed to defend my intelligence because I had injured my brain. Having such an odd-sounding voice just added to the challenge.

I tried to assist God numerous times by injecting my vocal cords with Botox. My brain injury causes my vocal cords to vibrate continuously. The Botox temporarily stops the vibration by numbing them. My voice would actually sound normal for a day or two. Then, as the drug continued to enter my vocal cords, I would lose all the volume in my voice. I had to speak right into your ear for you to hear me. Mom really put her lip-reading to task after my Botox injections.

The building crew at my new condominium bought me a whistle to blow as my "Come in!" whenever they knocked. At the time, they were working on my living room ceiling beams. I blew that whistle hourly for three weeks.

Once I tried to make a deal with God. I told Him I would stop smoking if He would cure my voice. On my way to the Vanderbilt Voice Clinic for another attempt at Botox injections, I smoked my last cigarette. I knew in my heart that God could not be bargained with, but I was so disgusted with my voice, it was worth a try. I was not at all surprised when my holy bargain did not work.

God knew it would take more than just concern for my health to get me to finally throw the cigarettes away. I had smoked through the training and running of two marathons, so I was clearly not concerned with it affecting my race time. Yet I finally gave up the habit at the slightest hope of getting my voice back.

Making an idol

My quest to regain the mobility and coordination that my brain injury had taken away became my full-time occupation. I spent hours every day performing the exercises my therapists had given me or practicing walking. If I got bored at a family gathering, I would excuse myself to the living room to perform my floor exercises for a second time that day.

My drive to walk normally again had taken over my life. I had made an idol out of my own mobility. I was coming dangerously close to putting my mobility ahead of God. He tells us in 1 Timothy 4:10 *That is why we labor and strive, because we have put our hope in the living God, who is the Savior of all people, and especially of those who believe.*

I was certainly one of those who believed, but I was relying on my own efforts to make it happen. It was now time to leave this strong aspiration in God's hands, where it should have been all along.

Dear Lord,

Thank You for giving me the courage and determination to make the best of this interruption in my life. I never really looked at or thought about handicapped people before. Now I think most of them are stronger than the average Joe. Many of them, just like me, had their life together and were moving forward with many plans. They may appear different in some obvious way, but they are thinking, feeling human beings. Forgive me for taking them for granted. Forgive me for not taking the time to notice.

Please watch over the many disabled people in our world. Inspire them to know and love You more, so that we may all be skipping and jumping and singing in your eternal kingdom.

And please forgive me for taking matters into my own hands and not trusting that you would work all things out in your timing.

Chapter 8

__BEING A MOTHER: THE EARLY YEARS__

Listen, my son, to your father's instruction and do not forsake your mother's teaching. They are a garland to grace your head and a chain to adorn your neck.

Proverbs 1:8-9

Andrew was just four years old when I moved back to Louisville. I did not see him before I left, since I was so stunned and shocked that Drew was sending me away. That was on November 10th. Andrew came to Louisville for Thanksgiving that year, the first of many times my dad would drive to Jackson, Tennessee to meet Drew half-way to pick up his grandson. I usually rode with him, but I skipped that first trip.

I was ecstatic to see Andrew! His grandparents, aunts, uncles and cousins made him feel he was part of a much bigger family than he was used to in Little Rock. He said two things on that trip that I will forever keep in my heart. "Mommy, I know I do not see you very much. But I still think about you every day." He said it casually, like he was telling me he wanted Froot Loops for breakfast. Then, a couple of days later, he told my mom, "Do not worry, Grandma. When you and Grandpa get too old to take care of Mommy, I will take care of her." I recalled his remarks many times to console myself those first few years when I wanted him by my side.

Andrew was used to being an only child. Having so many cousins, so thrilled to see him, was a new and wonderful surprise. When he was younger, my nephew Jack would frequently ask, "Aunt Mary, when is Andrew coming from *Arsanka* again?" He had twelve cousins, most of whom were younger than he was, and seemed to adore him. Andrew loved to entertain his cousins by doing a somersault as he walked into the room. He was always on cloud nine with so many family members in one place.

<u>Teaching him to pray</u>

When I was still living in Little Rock, I taught three-year-old Andrew an easy prayer that he could say every night. We knelt before the crucifix in his bedroom as I groped for the words, *God bless Mommy. God bless Daddy. God bless Andrew. God bless Torsha. And, dear Lord, thank you for a really good day.*

When Andrew was five years old, I tried to teach him the *Our Father*. After three nights of practice, he asked me if we could just say the *simple* prayer that night. When I inquired about what the *simple* prayer was, Andrew said, "You know! The 'Dear *Lord, thank you for a really good day'* prayer." He had been praying that prayer every night since he was three years old!

Sending Andrew to a Catholic elementary and high school was one of the few demands I made in my divorce settlement, since none of his Little Rock family was Catholic. Andrew was baptized a Catholic as an infant. I wanted to ensure that God was a part of his everyday life, if only in school. I thus agreed to finance Andrew's Catholic education even though Drew was his custodial parent.

It still breaks my heart that I was not there to parent him through those formative years. There were so many spiritual rituals I would have loved to pass on to him. Mostly, though, I wanted to be there to point out examples of God's hand in everyday occurrences. I wanted to pray with him!

I wanted to share his joy and excitement; his fears and frustrations. Aside from eight weeks of visitation annually, I was an absentee parent. It was difficult to watch my brothers and sisters enjoying or even disciplining their kids. That was a part of life that had been taken from me.

God knew what was best for Andrew, though. He allowed him a normal childhood free from the challenges of a disabled mother. It was horrible for me, but mothers always want what is best for their children, right? I have managed to keep a smile on my face, with a lump in my throat, for eighteen years now. I keep reminding myself that it is not about me. *Repeat. It is not about me.*

For the first few years, Andrew wanted me to magically go back to how I was before the accident, so that Drew would want me back in his life. As my life here in Louisville became more active, he asked me one day, "Mommy, you really would not go back to Daddy, even if you got better, would you?" I was glad I gave him the impression of having a full and happy life; at the same time, it broke my heart that he dreamed of his mommy and daddy being together again. It made me realize that this was not just hard on me.

Andrew had lost the mother that was supposed to minister to and care for him. He would be different from the other kids at school. Drew was and is a wonderful father, but he is not Andrew's mommy. Everyone needs a mommy. They listen to your feelings and comfort you when you are down. They get excited when you do something worthwhile. They encourage you, teach you and point you to God. Moms make everything okay again. I could not help him with his homework or take him to soccer practice, but I pledged to be the best long-distance mommy I could. I was reminded again that it is not about me.

I badgered my friends constantly about their children's lives. How much direction did they give them on school work? What time did they go to bed? How many hours a day did they spend with their friends? How did they determine if a friend was not a good influence on them? Then how did you approach the subject without being the bad guy? I wanted to know everything!

When Andrew was eight years old, his teachers excused him from class two days before the Thanksgiving holiday so he could spend a few more days with me in Louisville. He was responsible for all the homework he would miss. I was really excited to have him actually working on his studies at my house. I had visions of helping him with his homework and fixing him snacks while he worked. I was putting groceries away as he worked, when he turned towards me. "Mommy, would you please go in the other room? You are bugging me." So much for motherly guidance!

Christmas was always a real thrill when Andrew was younger. Santa Claus came to both Louisville and Little Rock. Since Louisville was his *vacation home* without school, it was a challenge to get him to bed without me, so I could put out all the Santa Claus gifts. The next morning, he would say, "Mommy, go check to see if he came!" On my return, "Did he come? Are there lots of presents? I want to go see!" Before he went flying through the house, I made sure both Mom and Dad were up to witness and film the celebration.

The Christmas before Andrew turned ten years old, all he wanted for Christmas was an iPod. I could not find one in Louisville, and I knew

Drew had had no luck either. Andrew kept telling me that if Santa did not bring the iPod to Louisville, he would bring it to Little Rock. I decided it was time to break the news about Santa Claus. When I told him Santa Claus was really Mommy and Daddy, he did not get it at first. He thought I was just expressing that Santa was loving and generous like a parent. "There is no Santa Claus, Andrew. Your dad and I buy those presents for you." His eyes got wide. "No way!"

Then I explained that the trick now was to keep pretending like he believed in front of all his cousins. Andrew loved games, and I told him this would be the best game he had ever played. When Drew called later that day, Andrew told him he knew *the secret.* Now he would get to keep that secret from all of his little cousins.

That Christmas will go down in the history books as one of his best childhood ones. Not only did he discover the secret that only *little kids* still believed, but his uncle Andrew, also known as Uncle A, surprised him with an iPod Nano on Christmas Day. Andrew called it the best of the best.

Time spent with Andrew was rare and special. We didn't have a typical mother/son relationship. From a very early age, Andrew was carrying and fetching things that my imbalanced body found difficult. He was all boy, yet I found ways we could interact over girly things. Andrew inherited my very fine, straight hair. We could spend hours in front of the mirror trying different gels and sprays to keep our hair coiffed and out of our eyes.

I watched with longing as other mothers walked through stores, holding their child's hand. I could not hold Andrew's hand because I was concentrating so earnestly on balancing my own body. Thankfully, that changed as he grew taller. Once Andrew's height equaled that of my walking cane, I could use his arm for stability.

At his young age, it wasn't practical to engage Andrew in deep conversation, but it was certainly rewarding to hear him belly-laugh over something silly that was happening. We were at Mom and Dad's once for dinner after I had gotten my own place. I suddenly let out a sneeze that shook my whole body. I quickly said, "God bless me!" Andrew laughed so hard, I thought he would cry. "That's what happens when you live by yourself too long." That made him laugh even harder.

The Varga family was an integral part of his visits to Louisville, and of developing my parenting skills. I looked to my siblings and their spouses for help and advice. My father, however, became Andrew's Louisville dad. He cared for him and disciplined him the same way he did his own children as we were growing up. Drew always remarked on how polite Andrew acted when he returned from Louisville.

As an only child with one parent, Andrew developed a sharp make-believe imagination. That was a behavioral issue my dad had never dealt with. Once, Andrew and I were riding in the back seat with Mom and Dad in the front. Andrew was making different kid noises while his action heroes were in the heat of a battle. I knew that the noise was bothering Mom and Dad. After a few minutes I turned to Andrew, asking, "Is he dead yet?" That stopped his antics for a few minutes, since he was laughing so hard.

Shopping became one of our favorite ways to spend time together. I could not play ball with him, but I could surely roll a shopping cart around the mall. Andrew knew I was good for a new toy, game or shirt. "Oh please Mommy, please! I will never ask for anything again!" until the next store. As a teenager, he became very label-conscious. It always had to be the right name brand. I found TJ Maxx to be the best store to quench his label hunger, while being nice to my pocketbook.

I tried to have things planned for every day he was here. "Mommy, could we just stay home and watch TV tonight? We can order a pizza."

Thank you God! That was music to my ears. When Andrew was about twelve years old, he explained to me that he came to Louisville to see me. He was happy just hanging out and seeing some good TV. Maybe it was just *me* that always wanted to be doing something.

I was sad when Andrew had to leave. For days I would wake up thinking he was in the next room. I would find myself missing my family too. It was a treat for the family when Andrew was in town. I would see or talk to them daily, but they went back to their family routines after he left; then it was just me again.

Dear Lord,

What a precious son You have given me! You know how much I want him with me all the time. It's not fair to him, though. He deserves a normal childhood. I cannot give him that. Not being able to drive anymore has become the biggest handicap I face. Children want to go, go, go, and now! Andrew is so very patient with me. Let that patience grow and serve him well as he gets older.

Thank You that my family and friends step up to help me keep Andrew entertained and challenged. Thank You for the positive role models that they are. Single parenting is hard; single disabled parenting is even harder. You knew I would need lots of help. You have given me the best.

Whenever gifts are called for, Andrew gives me crosses and religious plaques. I am glad he sees me as someone who puts You first in my life. I am so glad that he prays to You every night. Is that my influence or his school's influence? We both know it is not Drew's. That was a lousy thing to say. Forgive me. Please bless Drew and give him Your guidance in raising a godly son.

Chapter 9

My Lost Independence

Blessed are the poor in spirit, for theirs is the kingdom of heaven.

Matthew 5:3

There are many things to be thankful for since I had my brain injury. So many people have helped me to do things that I could no longer accomplish on my own. I have never been one to ask for help unless I had already discovered that I could not do it myself, yet there are many tasks that I simply cannot do anymore.

Giving up running was relatively easy, but not being able to drive remains a constant thorn in my flesh. When Paul asked God to take away the thorn in his flesh in 2 Corinthians 12:7, God responded, *My grace is sufficient for you, for my power is made perfect in weakness.*

I should have been eternally grateful just to be alive, and I was. It was going to take me a while to figure out why God saved me, though. I had lost so much! *Why do You not show me now, Lord, and save me a lot of time and mistakes?*

I attributed my lingering unhappiness to the loss of independence from not being able to move around like I had before. I wanted to reach beyond this unfortunate turn in my life, but it was much bigger than me. I did not like being defined by my brain injury. I was ashamed of being disabled. It made me feel like less of a person, and physically, I was!

Independent is how I would have described my youth and middle adulthood. I never stayed in one place for long, but would flit in and out to make an appearance and make sure I wasn't missing anything. I grew bored if I stayed somewhere too long.

My incapacity for driving put an end to my flitting in and out. Now I remain in one place until I'm summoned to leave. It is challenging for me to stand around at get-togethers. If I put too much weight on either leg, it will start cramping after a few minutes. I do best to keep moving or find a chair. For me, the ideal party floor plan includes bar-top tables to lean against while standing. Then I can stand on one leg when the other leg becomes sore. I can see everything that's going on, too. Being the handicapped lady in the corner chair is very isolating and humiliating.

I knew I had a brain injury, but I did not feel or think any differently than I did before my accident. Others treated me differently, though. They were very kind and overly helpful. I surely appreciated their efforts, but they bothered me at the same time. I hated looking like something was wrong with me! I needed to spend some more time working on acceptance of my physical limitations.

I went to a Charismatic Renewal Conference where priests were available to hear confessions. I have never been a regular in the confessional, but I figured I needed to confess this one out loud. I told the priest that it really bugged me that people were always offering to help me. I felt like a poster child for brain injury. I knew it was ungrateful of me, but I hated being pitied.

The priest told me I had been given a great gift. He said that I had been given the opportunity to help other people honor God by helping me. I would like to say that that insight immediately changed my outlook, but being a stubborn, prideful person has, unfortunately, always come easy for me. My attitude did not change overnight, but the priest's words stuck with me. I no longer reply with "No thank you. I can do it myself." That remark has been replaced with "Bless your heart!" If people are trying to honor God by helping me, the last thing I want to do is snipe at them.

Transportation problems

When I first had my brain injury, not being able to drive was not even an issue. Just getting into an automobile without losing my balance was a real victory. I did not yet have the balance to get a walker from the back seat of a car, let alone try to put it back in the car. Loading and unloading the walker became a real process for whoever was driving me.

Vertigo was also a problem in the early stages of my brain injury. Whenever I was moving unnaturally, as in a car, I became very dizzy and nauseated. Mom and Dad witnessed that first-hand when I threw up all over their back seat after a lovely dinner at my sister's house. I was terribly embarrassed and ashamed. Dad wanted to express his displeasure, but knew it would make me feel worse.

The reason I got nauseated was because my father was a very abrupt, jerky driver. He was always very safe, but that safety usually included many sudden stops. After I got sick, I hoped he would try a slower, steadier pace. Instead, Dad just took a bucket with him whenever I was in the car.

Always trying to find other alternatives for me, Dad took me down to the Paratransit Authority to arrange for transportation on their handicapped-accessible bus. Then I could arrange my own transportation to the health club or shopping, the only two places I went routinely. The Paratransit service is a valuable commodity for people who cannot drive. They operate twenty-four hours a day and seven days a week.

However, using that service required an extreme amount of patience. Batteries would go dead on my portable phone just waiting to make a reservation. The Paratransit service is a shared-ride service, so everyone with a reservation waits their turn to be picked up or dropped off. You allow them fifteen minutes on either side of your scheduled pick-up time to arrive. Then you have to allow them an hour and twenty minutes to get you to your destination. I could feel my blood pressure rising with every stop they made. Patience has never been a strong suit for me. *You do not drive anymore, Mary. Be grateful the Paratransit service is available to take you places at such a nominal fee. You will eventually get there. Think of the funny stories you will have to tell, too.*

Friends and family took me to social occasions, but I relied on the Paratransit service to take me to my health club during the week. I have often referred to my health club as my *home away from home* because it was my only link with the world outside of home. I saw friends and business associates of my family in a very relaxed, fitness-oriented environment. Members there were always open and friendly. Like people everywhere I went, they always seemed to look out for me. In addition to the many friendships I formed at my health club, they were also very instrumental in pointing me towards the fitness career I would eventually have.

I needed reliable transportation in order to work, so my four brothers stepped up to meet my needs. After running an advertisement and securing a driver for every weekday, my brothers would take turns paying my monthly driver expense, allowing me to hold on to the little revenue I had from working. I will explain my little business in a later chapter.

Having a driver not only allowed me to work, but to go to meetings, grocery-shopping, and errand-running like any normal, car-driving American. On top of that, the ladies and men who drove me became very good friends, since I spent more time with them during the day than any other friends or family members.

Thus my transportation problem was for the most part taken care of. That did nothing to eliminate my personal mobility problem, but it gave me the opportunity to be out in the world again, experiencing different people and places. Not being able to move around quickly anymore was beyond frustrating, but at least I was not stuck inside wondering what the rest of the world was doing.

Dear Lord,

I hate not being able to drive anymore! It limits my independence so much! Perhaps that is what You are trying to fix in me. Was I too independent before? I guess it is teaching me patience. But I don't like it...at all!

If I did drive, I would not see my friends or family as much. I would be off doing things myself...or trying to, anyway. Remind me of that when I start complaining again. I cannot physically do what I used to. I need other people to help me.

I spend so much time alone since I moved to my own place. I certainly spend more time thinking about and praying to You. Surprisingly, I am never lonely. I always feel You with me.

Thank You for giving me such active and useful days. Please find it in your heart to send me someone to relax and enjoy my evenings with.

Help me to always remember that You have inspired many people to make my life more manageable. Rather than being aggravated at my lack of independence, let me be joyful and grateful that so many others make my life more doable.

Chapter 10

ASHAMED OF MY PHYSICAL SELF

The LORD is a refuge for the oppressed, a stronghold in times of trouble.

Psalm 9:9

In the movie *Regarding Henry*, Harrison Ford played a top attorney who gets shot in the head during a drug store burglary. The movie tells the story of his life after a traumatic brain injury. He began medical treatment using a walker, but was soon walking normally with no assistance.

Most of Henry's brain damage was in the frontal lobes of the brain, considered to be the emotional control center and home to our personalities. People who suffer from injury to the frontal lobes may see changes in their short-term memory, judgment, spontaneity, language, and social behaviors.

My brain trauma was called a contrecoup injury, meaning that every area of the brain was affected. I still have slight difficulty with my short-term memory and a raspy, hoarse-sounding voice. Most of my injured brain cells were in the cerebellum, which controls balance and coordination, or the brain stem, which in turn controls breathing, heart rate, eye movements and swallowing, among others. If brains were computers, then the brain stem would be considered the motherboard of the brain. It controls everything. The more I read about brain trauma, the more I realized how blessed I was to still have a good, able mind and a good, strong heart.

Unlike in the movie, I did not have a good, stable body any more. It was, however, strong and toned, which was 100% due to my weight lifting and other exercises. I was coordinated enough to walk without tripping most of the time. Were my fine motor skills good? Don't make me laugh!

While we were watching *Regarding Henry*, Dad asked me if I would give up my memory if I could run a marathon or drive to work. I told him I couldn't work without a memory and that running would just have to be a pleasant memory. I would never give up my good mind for a properly functioning body; I would just keep praying for a medical breakthrough.

That said, I came to be ashamed of how my body moved. I hated looking so handicapped. Simple, everyday tasks became a challenge. Emptying the garbage, unloading the dishwasher, carrying things from one area to another: They all required balance that I did not have.

When unloading the dishwasher, I would consciously think: Dig your heels into the floor. Bend from your hip. Elevate your ribcage. Pull your ears back over your shoulders. Then as I went to put dishes in the cabinet, I thought *Steady! Steady!* It was a real process, but I felt victorious when it was accomplished.

Occasionally, people joked about how slow I was. I also knew that my slowness and my inability to drive kept me from being included in many social events. I felt like less of a person with my disabilities.

I was content with teaching seniors and working myself out every day. It gave my life a real sense of purpose. I thought that all the functional exercises I led in class would help improve my balance and walking gait outside of class. They did, *somewhat,* but holding my body in perfect alignment for so many hours left me physically exhausted by dinner.

My mind kept going, though. This book was written usually with an exhausted body, but a still very active mind. I had time to pray and read God's word. Netflix also became a source of comfort. I would alternate watching popular programs with spiritual programs to ensure I stayed grounded in my faith.

Even when I was exhausted, I held onto my treadmill hand rails as I practiced my walking gait and watched television programs or Christian DVDs. Joyce Meyer, Joel Osteen, and Father Cedric Peseigna's *Live with Passion* were three uplifting favorites.

It was no wonder I was thin. Even when tired, I constantly pushed my body to do things it did not find natural. Even when relaxing to watch TV, I was consciously holding my body in the right alignment with hips and hamstrings pushed into the chair, stomach sucked up, chest uplifted, and shoulder blades squeezed together.

As a personal trainer and senior fitness instructor, was my instruction ever going to rub off on me? I knew my brain was injured, but I still had all the determination and perseverance that carried me through years of distance running. I saw physical rewards from regular running. Was I ever going to see rewards from my balance exercises? The seniors in my classes said they did. Was I just being impatient?

From the time I had first used a walker in 1997, I loathed it! I looked so crippled! I felt that people were looking at the walker instead of me. They were being nice to the walker; not me. I also felt that my intelligence was always in question because of my funny-sounding voice.

I discovered firsthand what it felt like to be discriminated against, although family and friends looked out for me and even strangers were kind and helpful. However, my opinion on things was seldom solicited. When it was, I don't think anyone took it seriously. *Mary has a brain injury. How would she know?*

I was ashamed and embarrassed by my immobility. The fact that disability prompted the end of my marriage just compounded that feeling. I often felt like a *disability* survivor rather than a brain injury survivor.

Disability had become the thorn in my flesh that St. Paul spoke about in 2 Corinthians 12:7. *Therefore, **in** order to keep me from becoming conceited, I was given a thorn in my flesh, a messenger of Satan, to torment me.* The Bible never tells us what the thorn in Paul's flesh was, but he traveled around too much for it to be a balance issue. Automobiles hadn't been invented yet. I wonder if he was ashamed and embarrassed because of his thorn.

I still looked the same as I did before my brain injury. I prided myself on being fit and strong, but even my pretty smile and fashion-sense could not hide the fact that I walked like a zombie and moved about with extreme caution. I could not look people in the eye for fear of losing my balance.

I still remember one hurtful, but honest comment Andrew made when he was ten years old. He said, *Everybody loves you Mommy, but nobody wants to fool with you.* I thought of that statement often when planning activities. I tried never to have the same person *fooling with me* for two consecutive days. That worked out well in my professional life as I arranged a different person to drive me each day. They could relax and not have to deal with my disabilities on the other days.

I knew that Jesus did not give up on me when I became tired and frustrated. He would have left me a long time ago if that were the case. He wanted the best for me. I prayed always to know His will. He placed people in my life and gave me the uncanny strength to come this far. With great expectancy, I prayed that He would give me His second touch to make my life even more joyful and purposeful.

If I focused on bringing God glory and doing well for others, I discovered I had little time to concern myself with how others viewed my physical capabilities or my mental competencies. The questions became: *Can I make them smile? Can I make them laugh? Can I inspire them to become a better person? How can I give God credit for this?*

I found that making light of my own physical limitations put people at ease and even inspired them to make my journey more comfortable. People wanted to feel useful and helpful. I was the perfect vehicle for making their desires a reality.

I was raised to believe that religion is a very personal and private issue, so talking about my faith used to feel uncomfortable. The more I spoke of my answered prayers, though, the more comfortable I found others were in talking about theirs. We were not meant to keep God in a closet. I would love to put my disabilities in one and lock the door, but I would never want Almighty God closed behind a door. Just as I do with my dad, I count on God's guidance in every aspect of my life.

Dear Lord,

Thank You for being my refuge. Sometimes I feel that I am all alone in this world. I'm not included many times because of my limitations. I am just a burden. You know I detest my disabilities. There I go, complaining again! I believe You use my disabilities to allow others to honor You as they help me. You allow me to inspire others at the same time.

Please lead me to a place where I can be happily active and helpful. I feel that way when I'm teaching my exercise classes. I want Your second touch in this area of my life, Lord. Show me other ways to be involved where I don't need to bother others to do it.

Please keep reminding me that this life is not about me, but about You and Your glory. Keep prompting me when there's an opportunity to brag about all You have done for me and inspire others to reach out to You.

Chapter 11

THE WOUNDED HEALER

And we know that in all things God works for the good of those who love him, who have been called according to his purpose.

Romans 8:28

As a marathon runner and regular gym groupie, physical fitness was my life. I would show up late for social engagements in order to get my run in. All that changed when I suffered my traumatic brain injury in May 1997. I used to run an eight-minute mile; now I was trying to keep my balance with a rolling metal cage called a walker.

I was upset and baffled. Why had this happened to me? I had so much! Life as I knew it...was over. I knew it was an accident, but it was so hard! I decided that this was not going to get the best of me.

God gave me a spirit of courage and determination. I was now in training for something bigger than a simple, little marathon.

Is this what my life had become? I did not work nearly this hard training for distance races. Even though my balance disability kept me from running anymore, I discovered that equipment, like an elliptical or a treadmill with handles could help me keep my aerobic fitness. Sit-ups, pushups and weight lifting required no balance, so I had no excuse for not doing them.

I was getting a sandwich for dinner at Subway one night. The manager opened the door for me as I was walking out to get on my scooter. "Do you mind if I ask you a nosy, personal question?" I smiled as I thought, *Here it comes again!* "Of course not. What did you want to know?" "How do you stay so incredibly fit?" he asked. I laughed and said, "Oh, that's easy. I run." The manager looked at me like I was nuts! "I can't run normally anymore because of my balance, but I can really get my heart pumping if I hold on to the handles of a treadmill."

During all my years of recuperation, I remained a gym groupie. As I watched the personal trainers working with their clients, I knew I was as fit as they. I didn't have to walk to write a fitness plan, or demonstrate proper use of exercise equipment. I decided this would be my new purpose, and I started studying for the personal training certification exam immediately.

My previous career as a pharmaceutical sales representative gave me an understanding of the body's anatomy and physiology, but memorizing new terms was very hard for me. My memory wasn't as good as I thought it was. Perhaps that was my brain injury, or perhaps my mind had become lazy from not studying for so many years. Whatever the reason, I had to take the exam twice before I passed the certification.

Today I am a certified personal trainer. My health club immediately put me on their payroll. However, in this profession, if you cannot obtain the clients, you do not work. Who was going to choose me with a club full of able-bodied trainers? My marketing background went right out the window. How do you promote a trainer with a balance and voice impairment? All that training and studying! Had I done the wrong thing? How could I promote myself? It seems the Lord had a different plan for me, and His plan surfaced only after I stopped telling Him all the reasons why it would not work out.

I am personally comforted and challenged when I read Moses speaking in Exodus 4:10. *Moses said to the Lord, "Pardon your servant, Lord. I have never been eloquent, neither in the past nor since you have spoken to your servant. I am slow of speech and tongue."* I knew God didn't need perfect speaking ability to help me touch the lives of others. I truly believed that God had put this dream in my heart. How would he make it a reality?

A woman from the Vocational Rehabilitation office suggested I teach group exercise classes in senior homes. Voc Rehab even bought me a portable sound system with a microphone. The microphone helped the seniors to hear my soft voice over the oldies music I used in class. Over time, I was able to add more classes. I started out teaching muscle toning and flexibility. Then I added more and more balance exercises. Balance work is very important for older people, and for me, too! The exercises I teach help me as much as they do my students. My years as a physical therapy patient gave me lots and lots of cues to use when I teach my classes.

A personal trainer—on a walker? That's not something you see every day. While my students aren't athletes or body builders any more, working with seniors gives me an audience that appreciates what I have overcome through regular exercise. I am able to encourage them beyond what they thought they were capable of.

My disabilities do not embarrass me or make me feel ashamed when I am teaching. They have led me to a new purpose in life; inspiring and encouraging those I serve. Many times I have heard myself using the same verbal cues with my classes that my physical therapists used while trying to get my body moving like it did before my accident. *Elevate your rib cage. Bring your hips forward. Squeeze your shoulder blades together.* Sometimes I sound like a broken record.

My local newspaper did a story about the classes I teach. It gave recognition to some of the seniors in the class and celebrated how they were able to get stronger while having a good time in the process. A friend in the marketing and advertising business designed a logo and web page for my little business, called SilverStrength. He did all this out of the goodness of his heart, as did my brother's friend who did all the legal work for my business trademark. My disability seemed to bring out the kindness and goodness in people.

God tells us in Romans 12:21 , *Do not be overcome by evil, but overcome evil with good.* My new purpose as a *wounded healer* uses the issues I've struggled with to motivate and encourage the seniors in my class. By showing them the exercises I've done to regain my mobility and strength, I have shown them ways to maintain their own.

To continue living independently, these seniors need to keep their bodies moving on a regular basis, just like I do. I help them keep their bodies in the proper alignment to make the tasks of everyday living easier. If caught slouching in my class, they are sure to hear me say, *Elevate your ribcage* for the 15th time!

Occasionally, a senior in one of my classes will let me know they are walking better or able to climb stairs since starting my classes. It seems to give them confidence that they can have mastery of their body moves through practice and proper execution of the move. As I lead the classes, I am practicing the proper body moves for myself too. I get a free physical therapy session every time I teach a class! My body moves have become more and more fluid and my balance is better since I began teaching. My body is exhausted by the end of the work day, though. Holding myself in good posture for several hours still does not feel natural. Is *this ever going to become natural?*

Improved muscle tone and flexibility are not the only benefit of taking my classes. It is also a great opportunity for the seniors to build camaraderie with the other residents. We share fashion tips, food recommendations and current events, all the while commiserating about why we have to exercise. We laugh, joke, and truly enjoy each other's company. I wake up excited to see them every day. Teaching these seniors has really enriched my life!

I look forward to going to work every day. Since May 10, 1997, (my accident) I have relied on people's assistance to get around in life, and I still do to some degree. What a boost it is to my confidence to have others watching my moves to help them get around more gracefully.

The majority of my pupils have better mobility than I do, yet they rely on my instruction for the proper execution of movement of their joints and muscles. One day a newspaper photographer was filming my class. I got nervous and lost my balance. I sat down immediately, as did my entire class. I still laugh thinking about it. They surely do follow their instructor's every move!

I have found my new purpose in leading these classes for seniors. I show them how to remain strong and flexible; they show me a wonderful outlet for helping people again. These ladies and men have become like a second family to me. I seek their advice on things. They watch out for me. My days of being a long-distance runner were taken away to make room for a new and more meaningful purpose. My race time is slower now, but much more rewarding.

Dear Lord,

Thank You for giving me the opportunity to enrich these seniors' lives through regular exercise. I forgot how good it feels to be needed by people. Thank You for letting me see this part of life again.

I still require assistance in many other areas of my life, but I get such a rush from giving help during my classes.

Maybe someday I will live in one of these assisted-living homes. I can have my own nice apartment when I want to be alone, but be surrounded by other people for meals and other activities during the day. Perhaps I can even get a break on rent if I keep teaching classes.

My life has been greatly uplifted by leading these classes. Thank You for showing me the value of reaching out to others.

Chapter 12

MY INNATE DESIRE TO WORK

For we are God's handiwork, created in Christ Jesus to do good works, which God prepared in advance for us to do.

Ephesians 2:10

At fifteen years of age, I donned what I perceived as appropriate work attire and walked from my home to Steak & Shake to fill out an application for employment. That was a jaunt of about one and a half miles, most of it on a busy thoroughfare. When I arrived, the manager told me they would not hire anyone under the age of sixteen. I was crushed!

Couldn't I have called first? Couldn't I have found someone to drive me? Of course I could have.

Long before my innate desire to work surfaced, my inborn impatience was rampant. I had a good idea and I wanted to follow up on it right now. My impatience would cost me an hour of needless walking that day. I have since learned to mention my plans to someone else to avoid doing something stupid or unnecessary.

I badly wanted to work! Money was never the issue. I was blessed to grow up in a family that provided for all my basic needs. The need to be needed and useful was my prime motivator. I will admit that wearing fashionable clothing kept me looking forward to the work day as well.

Over the years, I have learned that work requiring a lot of physical movement really ignites me. From the very first road race I ran, I was addicted to improving my physical strength and agility. I taught aerobic dance classes for the employees of a local hospital when I worked in their Human Resources department. I taught back-to-back classes for nursing staff and then business office personnel. It was an enjoyable way for employees to come together after work to relax and get in a workout before going home for the day. I would spend hours in my parents' basement choreographing exercise routines to music in front of three full-length mirrors. I did that to ensure my moves were understandable and could be easily followed. It never occurred to me that those aerobic dance classes I taught would be the precursor for the business, SilverStrength, that I now operate. It appears God was directing my path even way back then.

I worked in retail sales, hospital administration, and pharmaceutical sales prior to my brain injury. All of those careers called for quick communication skills and effortless mobility. Remember that I am no longer quick on my feet. None of those professions were a match for a lady with a balance disability. So what did I do? I studied to become a Certified Personal Trainer. Let me explain before you laugh.

Doctors and therapists have told me that I could accomplish most of the moves I wanted to perform with practice, practice, and more practice. Every class I teach becomes a physical therapy session for me. As the instructor, I'm always setting an example for the class: how to sit and stand tall, move with precision, and breathe deeply. I have to keep my body in perfect alignment when I'm leading a class. That is usually two classes a day on Monday through Friday. After six years of teaching, I've proven that I can move correctly in class. God tells us to *wait expectantly* for the answer to our prayers. Now I'm just waiting and expecting that it will filter over to my moves the rest of the day.

Whatever job I had in life became a part of my identity. That has been especially true in my profession as a personal trainer. I've seen people's lives change by improving their confidence in how their bodies move. I've passed on to my classes the messages passed on to me as I struggled through my rehabilitation. Never give up! Keep adjusting, correcting, and practicing until your body moves like you want it to move. More than any other career I've had, working with seniors has made me feel needed and useful. It is a joy to go to work every day.

Some people know from a very early age what they've been called to do with their life. I was not one of them. It took me four different careers and a brain injury before I felt prompted by God. In Colossians 3:23 God tells us, W*hatever you do,* **work** *at it with all your heart, as* **work***ing for the Lord, not for human masters.*

Are you serious, a personal trainer? I did not have the able body for it, but I made up for it with passion. God knew that being afflicted with physical challenges would inspire me to do whatever I had to do to overcome them. Now I not only have an innate desire to work, I have a newfound passion for helping others to overcome their own physical limitations. Sometimes, when lying in bed at night, I create exercises in my mind that would be helpful to my classes. I try not to do that when I have an early morning meeting; the mental energy I expend leaves me unable to sleep.

I know what you're thinking. *You're disabled. Why do you even want to work? Why don't you just relax and let the government support you?* I work because it allows me to do something useful with my day. It gives me the chance to be out in the world. It allows me to help others as I have always been helped.

Galatians 6:2 tells us to *carry each other's burdens, and in this way you will fulfill the law of Christ.* I am happy to be in a position from which I can actually offer assistance to people. God has taken care of me through a very arduous battle. He did it through many caring people. I am delighted to join them now in helping others instead of being the one in need of help. Don't get me wrong! I still need lots of help. It is, however, gratifying to have abilities that I can offer to others.

Dear Lord,

Thank You for putting the drive to work in me. Please let my motivation be to bring You glory, and not just to see the works of my hands. We both know that no one would've blamed me if I had just thrown in the towel with my brain injury. I knew You were expecting more from me. It feels so right to use the abilities You have given me to encourage and inspire other people.

Thank You for not giving up on me. Thank You for prospering my efforts.

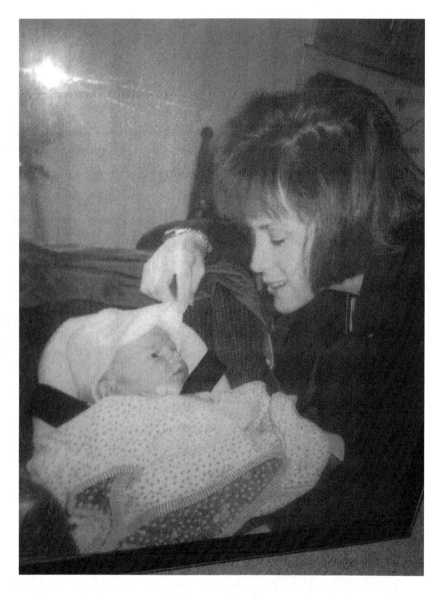

This photograph is of my son Andrew (2 months old) and me before the accident that caused the traumatic brain injury.

Chapter 13
THE AUTHOR OF MY STRENGTH

But those who hope in the LORD will renew their strength. They will soar on wings like eagles; they will run and not grow weary, they will walk and not faint.

Isaiah 40:31

Extraordinary strength has been a much appreciated character trait my whole life. Not to worry; Mary can handle it. Drew used to say I had more strength in my little finger than most people have in a lifetime. My innate strength became a valuable commodity after my journey with brain injury and disability began. Without balance, simple everyday movements became a challenge. Notice I did not say *chore*. Challenges were to be mastered or overcome. *Chores* were just to be put up with. I never stopped trying to overcome my physical limitations.

I thanked Jesus for being my model in dealing with the challenges that I faced daily. On the road to Calvary, Jesus fell three times with His cross. Each fall brought more pain. I suppose I had the Lord beat on the number of falls. My falls were usually not painful, though, just embarrassing. At least I understood the mental pain of humiliation Jesus went through. I had little control over my falls. The Lord went to the cross by choice for you and me. I felt very connected with Him in my suffering. Hebrews 12:2 says, *Looking unto Jesus, the author and finisher of our faith, who for the joy that was set before Him endured the cross, despising the shame, and has sat down at the right hand of the throne of God.* I thought of Jesus as the author of my strength. He knew what I was going to face in this life. He knew the strength of character I would need to keep moving forward, so He gave me a double portion of His strength.

Determination and perseverance were usually two of the by-products of having strength. I had been blessed with ample amounts of both. But that strength needed to be harnessed for God's purposes. Strength of character is a noble thing. Having a strong will can be either a positive asset, or a pathway to planning and doing evil. I needed to stay in constant contact with the Lord to make sure my strength was on the right path.

I learned much from struggling with my physical limitations and my personal setbacks. If you can persevere through the hard parts, you become stronger. The struggles eventually become old news, and old news is easier to handle because you have taught yourself how to deal with it.

I had a car wreck resulting in a brain injury, and because of poor balance, I cannot walk very well—*old news.* My husband divorced me because he could not deal with my handicaps any longer—*old news.* My son has not lived with me since he was four years old. It is painful, yet it is still *old news.* I have learned how to live with it.

As life became easier, and good things began to come my way, I got really nervous. I did not believe that the Lord who walked with me through my tunnel would ever abandon me. Rather, I was afraid I would turn my back on Him. I feared I would think the good was all from my hard work and effort, instead of His grace and love for me.

What I referred to as faith, people called my strength. I guess the two do go hand in hand. It required faith and strength to do the right thing when others around you were taking the easy path. It required faith and strength to admit being wrong, even if others excused such behavior as understandable under the circumstances.

I saw this personally in my relationship with Drew when I felt the Holy Spirit prompting me to forgive him. I did not really need to do that, humanly speaking. We lived in different cities, and as far as I was concerned, he had already won *our battle*. He had our son. He had remarried. He shared life with Andrew in a way I could only dream of, yet I needed to forgive him for short-circuiting my life and taking away my family...I knew Drew was racked with guilt. How could he not be? He was a good man who was knowingly hurting the woman he had loved. Perhaps that is why he referred to me before the accident as the *old Mary,* and since the accident as the *new Mary.* In his mind, he was just throwing away the new model. Drew did not want this life for me even as I did not, but I did not have a choice about living with it; he did. I said I would never have thrown our marriage away, but who was I to judge? Only God knows what I would have done in the same circumstances.

For if you forgive other people when they sin against you,

your heavenly Father will also forgive you

That is what God tells us in Matthew 6:14.

I decided the right thing to do for both our lives was to forgive Drew. I watched a TV program on forgiveness one Sunday morning. It emphasized the importance of reaching out to the person who wronged you, telling them you forgave them. *Do You really want me to call Drew, Lord? Can't I just forgive him in my heart?* I prayed about it, but didn't need trumpet blasts to know the answer to that one. So I called him. "I do not know if this will mean anything to you, Drew. I was watching a program on forgiveness. I think I forgave you years ago, but this program said it was not complete until I confronted you with my mercy." There was a long pause. Then Drew said at last, "That means so much to me. You are the strongest woman I have ever known."

My attitude towards Drew changed that day. I no longer felt he was just trying to hurt me more when he made decisions I did not agree with. He loved Andrew as much as I did. I truly forgave him for changing the course of my life. Hard as it was, he was simply an instrument God had used to bring me to my ultimate destiny, which still remains to be revealed. By forgiving Drew, I freed myself to go forward with no hurt feelings.

Drew was not expecting it. It was a most liberating feeling, which surprised me too. Now I could put it all behind me and move forward to wherever God was leading me.

Dear Lord,

Thank You for finally showing me the power of forgiveness. As the author of my strength, I wish You could have gotten it through my thick head years earlier. That is what You would have done. Forgive me for being so slow to the punch.

Thank You for helping me to harness my strength for Your good purposes. Thank You for giving me such delight in helping other souls. You continually show your love and compassion for me. I thought I was going to live out my life as a poor and lonely handicapped lady. You have shown me differently. When I read Your word and come to You regularly, I feel refreshed. Most importantly, I do not feel alone. You are always with me! You have given me opportunities to be an encourager and an inspiration to others.

I adore You!

Andrew (in his young teens) and I at his very first Brain Ball.

Chapter 14

BEING A MOTHER: TEENAGER AND YOUNG ADULT

Can a mother forget the baby at her breast and have no compassion on the child she has borne? Though she may forget, I will not forget you!

Isaiah 49:15

Andrew was a teenager like most others, I presume. He was very much into himself and his friends. Parents were very *uncool.* He would spend a week with me rolling his eyes every time I asked a question. "You ask too many questions, Mom!" Asking questions was the only way to know what was going on in his life. Drew never felt the need to consult me about Andrew, unless there was a bill from his school that needed to be paid. We could have been a real team where Andrew was concerned, but he was Andrew's custodial parent; he did not want or need my opinion. It was very humiliating! Sometimes I felt like his Little Rock life was in competition with the little time he was able to spend in Louisville. I would always inquire about his dad and the people I knew from Little Rock. That was such a long-ago time in my life, though. I always had to remind myself that it was the only home Andrew had ever known. Unfortunately, it was the place of my most unpleasant memories.

Drew remarried a few years after our divorce. I made a big deal about it when Andrew came to visit. We went to the mall to pick out a special gift from him for their upcoming nuptials. Andrew was totally uninterested in the gift-buying process. I do not know if he was just being a teenager, or if he was doing it for my benefit.

Drew's new wife's name was Heidi. She was a really nice lady! After she married Drew, I received my first-ever birthday and Mother's Day gifts from Little Rock. Ladies know how important it is to acknowledge those days. It had always hurt my feelings that Drew did not recognize them, but perhaps that is just the way men behave. The biggest accomplishment of the gift giving was that Andrew took such pride in what he was giving me.

The first time I met Heidi, Andrew was not even a teenager yet. I had flown to Little Rock to finally catch one of his baseball games. Heidi came over to Drew's house after the game. Andrew and I were sitting on the couch watching a movie. She got down on her knees and grabbed my arm with both hands. "How are you, Mary?" Andrew just shrugged. We exchanged a few nice comments, but the whole time I was thinking, *What has Drew told her about me?* At that point I was still convinced that Drew thought I was half retarded. So I could only imagine how he had described his brain-injured ex-wife.

Heidi had a woman's perspective on things and she intuitively knew what I so longed to know about my son. For the first time since my divorce, I was actually getting information on how Andrew was doing. It came via email usually, but I attributed that to my voice. It was very difficult to follow me for any length of time on the telephone. I could express myself much more easily and fluidly by email.

She may not have even realized it, but Heidi had introduced Andrew to the sheer joy of giving. He was very excited to see what I thought about his Mother's Day gift. Heidi told me he had labored over which type of dishes to get me. I felt such delight in knowing he picked them out with my taste in mind.

You have heard about the *terrible twos,* but they were nothing compared to the *terrible teens.* Andrew was a good kid with a heart of gold, but like most teenagers, he thought his parents were old-fashioned and totally un-cool. It is hard enough to live in the same house with a teen; imagine being a parent to a teen three states away! Andrew did not just stay in his room. He would not answer the phone when I called. I felt completely isolated from him.

Friends routinely asked me how Andrew was doing. I felt ashamed when I was actually honest with them. "I have no idea!" I was not being a bad mother, but felt very much like an unnecessary one. Drew and Heidi had their own set of issues with a teenage son. Drew never wanted me to be a part of them. I would like to think the best of him. He did not want to concern me with their issues. Unfortunately, I usually felt it was insinuated that it was none of my business. He was the custodial parent. Butt out!

I tried not calling Andrew for awhile. I knew he would never call me. Then I would worry that he thought I was ignoring him. *You are the adult here, Mary. So what if he is icy on the phone? At least you let him know you still love him and think about him.* I had never felt so insignificant in my life. My own son did not have time for me! I was sure most mothers felt this way occasionally, but it only added to my fear that no one had time for this *nice little disabled lady.* How could I remedy this situation? I wanted to fix it. How do I fix this mess? There must be something I can do! *Be still and know that I am God.* I was finally able to leave this one in His hands.

The time came for Andrew to graduate from high school. If he had lived close to Louisville, my family would have been there in force, but no one could make the trip to Little Rock. I decided I would not go either, since I require someone to hold my hand for balance in order to move at a normal pace. Since my family was not going, I did not want to rely on Heidi or Drew to get me around. We would just have a big graduation party when Andrew came to Louisville.

Andrew was disappointed, but understood my predicament. I actually got choked up talking to Drew. "I cannot believe I am missing my own son's graduation." Drew told me not to give up hope yet; he would call me later.

The next day, I received an email from Heidi saying they wanted to pay for my plane ticket and would make sure that Andrew was always around to escort his mom. I was so touched that I insisted on getting my own plane reservation, if they would cover the hotel cost. Flying is always an adventure for me. I brought lots of tip money, since I was always asking for help. I was going to Andrew's graduation, though. I was so excited! Andrew seemed very relieved that I had decided to make the trip.

I went straight to the airport from teaching a senior exercise class wearing yoga pants and a sweat jacket. I had my outfit for Andrew's graduation party in my suitcase. My flight was late and Andrew made a wrong turn in traffic when picking me up. Those two incidents gobbled up the hour I had to change clothes. So I met all of his friends and their families in the same workout attire I had been wearing since 9:00 that morning.

Andrew was on Cloud nine! Everyone was there to celebrate him. He was thrilled and moved when I read the poem my brother Paul wrote for his graduation. Due to my raspy voice, I was very relieved that the whole crowd seemed to understand every word I said. It was a great poem entitled "Head Start." It actually could have applied to any of the graduates present that night. Uncle Paul is a very gifted writer.

The next day Andrew took me to lunch by the Arkansas River at Faded Rose. It was one of my favorites when I lived in Little Rock. Then he drove me around to show me all his favorite spots. "You really do love this place, don't you?" I asked. Andrew replied, "It's my home!"

My brother Dan drove up from Dallas for the graduation ceremony. I was so happy that Dan made the trip. The Varga family had made an appearance, after all. Drew, Heidi, Dan and I went back to my hotel for drinks after the graduation. Dan and Drew carried on like long lost friends. Celebrating Andrew's graduation brought our families together for the first time since our divorce. It was a bittersweet evening.

I badly wanted Andrew to choose the University of Kentucky for college. It would be the first time since he was four years old I would be living in the same state with him. My brother Paul was gracious enough to drive him up to Lexington to tour the campus. I flew Andrew's cousin Sam Varga in from Dallas to accompany them. Sam had gone to UK before moving with his family to Dallas. He was also the cousin that Andrew had looked up to since he was a little boy. Paul left after the tour, leaving Sam to show Andrew the UK night life, along with tailgating at a Wildcat football game.

Since I was a UK alumna, Andrew received a Legacy scholarship. Then UK really surprised me by giving him in-state tuition since I lived in Kentucky. I thought that sealed the deal since the only other college Andrew was considering was his father's alma mater, Westminster College. Westminster is a small, private liberal arts college much smaller and much more expensive than UK. One of Drew's friends, also a Westminster alumnus with close ties to the college, secured a Presidential scholarship for Andrew. That put Westminster's tuition right in line with UK's cost. So it was all Andrew's choice. Did he want big or did he want small?

Andrew was impressed with the University of Kentucky, but somehow I knew in my heart he was going to choose Westminster. Andrew had always been a big fish in a small pond. I feared UK would completely overwhelm him. He chose Westminster. He could certainly be a big fish there. I am sure calling me was something he dreaded doing. "Hardest part is over," I teased him. "You just have to break the news to all of your cousins now." They adored their big cousin Andrew. Having him close would have been a dream come true. It made me feel better to have others to share my disappointment with.

Louisville did not see Andrew that summer before he left for college. He had a full time job as a waiter at the Little Rock Country Club. Occasionally I would text him, "I would like a grilled chicken on whole wheat bread. No mayo please." Once he texted me back, "Not even funny!" I suppose he got a lot of unusual menu requests.

When the weekend to move him to school finally happened, I felt horrible that I could not be a part of it. He needed strong arms and quick feet to get his dormitory room in tip-top shape. He kept me abreast with text pictures and videos. Drew and Heidi did a fabulous job getting his dorm room set up in style. I am sure they miss him even more than they thought they would. He was the focus of their life for many years.

A strange and wonderful thing happened after Andrew was in college. He started answering his phone, actually being happy to talk to his mother. Will it last? He needs to feel connected to people who love him right now. Will we all go back to being *uncool* parents again once he feels settled? Maybe this is a whole new beginning.

I felt like the true mother of a teenager when Andrew called me one night from college *just to talk*. He hasn't wanted to *just talk* on the phone in nineteen years. What was the real reason for his call? He needed money. He had overextended himself at the Kappa Alpha spring formal and had fifty dollars left to last him until the semester ended in three weeks.

I had given him nine months of one hundred dollars a month for gas money as a high school graduation gift. He had only used four months at that point, so I gladly sent him a few more months of gas money. I laughed as I told him I felt like a real collegiate mom now.

Andrew adored Westminster. I'm so happy now that he chose a smaller college. Unfortunately, a long-festering problem that Andrew had with mental focus showed up with a vengeance. He was such a bright kid that keeping high grades came naturally for him through elementary and most of high school.

When he really had to put his mind to college courses, his habitual daydreaming became more intense. His doctor said Andrew had used daydreaming as a coping mechanism for years. Now it was interfering with his scholarship.

All these years, I thought mine was the only life affected by my brain injury. The consequences of it had clearly affected my son's life too. My absence in Andrew's life had produced side effects. It made him different from other kids. Until his dad had remarried, he had had no mother figure in his life. Have Drew and I ruined his happy childhood? We've certainly caused a daydreaming problem. Time to intensify my prayers for Andrew!

Dear Lord,

I forget sometimes that You love Andrew even more than we do. Let him have a happy and normal college experience at Westminster. Guide his decisions now that he is away from home. Help him to find the right area of concentration in his studies.

He has a girlfriend and has joined a fraternity. Help him to balance his social calendar with his academic pursuits. Above all, let him see Your hand in his life. His reasoning mind is full of questions about Your place in his life. Let Your Holy Spirit guide him into all truth and lead him back to you.

I always thought that Andrew led a happy life despite the mistakes of his parents. Please give him the determination to stay focused in the real world...and to make You a part of that world.

Andrew with Mom and Dad at his high school graduation.

Chapter 15

<u>JOINING IN AND GIVING BACK</u>

Give, and it will be given to you. A good measure, pressed down, shaken together and running over, will be poured into your lap. For with the measure you use, it will be measured to you.

Luke 6:38

The first few years I was back in Louisville, I concentrated on improving my mobility, staying in touch with Andrew, and deepening my relationship with God. I became a voracious reader of mostly spiritual books. Up until that point in my life, I had experienced so much of God's goodness, and my brain injury was the first time my faith had really been tested. It made me realize what a blessed life I had always had. Many others facing my sort of tragedy did not have the family support or the financial support to seek the rehabilitation they needed.

However, during this time I still felt very alone and different from everyone else. I felt like Mary had been taken away from me. The same friends and family that used to laugh with me or roll their eyes at me now looked at me with pain in their eyes. Sometimes they would not look at me at all. Perhaps there was something to the *old Mary/new Mary* theory that Drew always held. He thought the *old Mary* was dead. She was not really dead, though, just buried deep inside a crippled body.

One day my mother brought her friend, Philomena, over to see my new apartment. That apartment was my first attempt at asserting my independence again after living with Mom and Dad for four years. Mom and Phil were coming up with ideas to get me out of my now solitary existence. Phil mentioned a friend of hers whose daughter also had a brain injury. She told me that every month a group of brain injury survivors would meet for dinner together. I was intrigued at the thought of meeting them. I had never even met anyone outside my initial hospital recovery that had a brain injury.

The name of this dinner group was Headliners. The group met the second Wednesday of every month at a different family restaurant. I walked with a walker at the time. It surprised me that so few other brain injury survivors did. Was this a promise of life to come, or was it just a difference in the type of brain injury?

When I came home from dinner that night, I listed everyone's name and hair color/style on a napkin. I wanted to remember their names next month, and I was not going to trust my short-term memory. It was nice to be with others from a similar situation, but none of us seemed to have the same deficits. I was beginning to understand the truth that every brain injury is different.

We also had a monthly dinner called Girls' Night Out. That was a group of eight to ten survivors, usually with their mothers. My mother was already having mobility issues of her own by that point, so I never felt inclined to invite her. I felt like an outsider in this group at first, but have since found myself always looking forward to our time together. A group of ladies can always find something to gab about. It was relaxing to be with ladies who understood my deficits and liked being around me anyway.

I could not have participated in either of these social groups without my friend, Bev. Her daughter Colleen also had a traumatic brain injury. Colleen and I had both graduated from Assumption high school, although several years apart. Her mother, Bev, was not only attentive to Colleen's physical needs, but mine as well. Every group needs someone to take responsibility to make sure that all goes smoothly for everyone in attendance. In this group her name was Bev. She also provided me with transportation to most of these activities.

I joined another support group called 8-9-10. They were described to me as being higher functioning. Most of the individuals in 8-9-10 did not have physical limitations like mine. They were more concerned with cognitive issues such as memory and reasoning. With my walker and balance issues, I felt like an outcast even among brain injury survivors. The group consensus seemed to be that they appeared normal, but felt different because of their brain injury. *Dear Lord, Please let me appear normal someday!*

I made some special friends in these groups, but we rarely socialized outside of our monthly time together. We all had brain injuries, but otherwise did not have many shared interests. Most of us had to plan our transportation wherever we went. That made getting together at another time nearly impossible, yet we congregated every month like clockwork.

Brain Injury Alliance of Kentucky

I had been back in Louisville for over a year before I was introduced to a group that has become an integral part of my life. The Brain Injury Alliance of Kentucky (BIAK) provides support and advocacy for individuals whose lives have been affected by brain injury. If my accident had occurred in Louisville, they would have been involved with me from my initial hospital stay. As it was, I was a transplant to town three years after my brain injury.

My first contact with BIAK was when I called their executive director to see if they could help me with a fundraising gala my family wanted to host. It was then I discovered that everything related to brain injury needed the endorsement of BIAK and my brother, Dan, was on the board of directors. Why did someone not tell me this before I made this call with my goofy-sounding voice?

I continued to use my altered voice to call family, friends, and associates in an effort to get committee members for this fundraising gala. Dan's wife, Kim, came up with the original idea for this gala. She thought the name *Brain Ball* had a catchy ring to it. I was just doing what had always come naturally for me; planning a party. I did not realize I needed board approval to orchestrate it.

You have heard the saying, "It takes a village." The Brain Ball was definitely one of those endeavors. Once I had gotten an affirmative response from Brain Ball committee members, we needed a place to meet, refreshments for the meeting, and most importantly, a date and venue for the Brain Ball.

Thank you Lord, for a family that stands with me! My brothers used their business and personal contacts to gather sponsors, find a band and ensure a good attendance at that first Brain Ball. I used my own business contacts from my former life in Louisville to design our first Brain Ball invitation.

The big night finally came. The Brain Ball committee worked hard all day to get the ballroom at the Olmstead House ready for our big event. My sister-in-law, Kim, had designed the entry to the gala with twinkling lights and papier maché to give the appearance of a human brain and spinal cord. A recording played, "You are now entering the human brain. Enter the spinal column."

The silent auction operated during cocktail hour and dinner. I saw many friends I had not seen since returning to Louisville. BIAK raised more money than at any previous fundraiser. After the dinner, I was presented with the Inspiration Award for all my work and my family connections that inspired the creation of the Brain Ball. It was indeed a magical night.

BIAK has continued to host the Brain Ball every fall. It has become a regular on the city's social calendar and a tried-and-true fundraising gala for BIAK. It draws people together from all over Louisville.

After the first Brain Ball, the Executive Director of BIAK telephoned to tell me I had been nominated to serve on their board of directors. I was excited and a little scared. I saw it as a chance to help other brain injury survivors, but was worried that my voice and my lack of exposure to the business world would make me ineffective. Shyness has never been a problem for me, but sounding stupid and asking too many questions has been a constant fear with my speech impairment (medically defined as dysphasia). I was however, able to bring a brain-injury-survivor perspective that other board members could not.

God tells us in Hebrews 13:16, *Do not neglect to do good and to share what you have, for such sacrifices are pleasing to God.*

I felt most effective in speaking to other brain injury survivors and BIAK provided me with opportunities to do just that over the years. Whether meeting new survivors in the hospital, speaking to small groups, or participating in the annual walk-a-thon, I am most fulfilled when I feel like I am providing hope to others who are facing the same challenges as me.

Most recently, I have started teaching my SilverStrength exercise classes at two of the NeuroRestorative centers. NeuroRestorative provides community-based rehabilitation programs for people of all ages with brain and spinal cord injuries and other neurological challenges. The residents are not seniors, but brain injury survivors like me.

Most of them are younger than me, so I get to play classic rock music instead of classic oldies. It is rewarding to be with other brain injury survivors and to be able to encourage their physical fitness. Even more than the seniors I teach, this group likes to move! I've actually gotten winded leading the class.

I've discovered helping other people to be the most immediate way to find joy and solace in my circumstances. Seeing the hope and determination in a survivor's eyes as I demonstrate a better way for them to execute an exercise brings me a feeling of fulfillment. They really are paying attention. They really do want to make the best of their brain-injured mobility.

I could tell they were evaluating me at the first class. After hearing me talk and seeing how I moved, they must've decided I was just one of them and not some proper or egotistical personal trainer. We're all in this together.

Dear Lord,

There really are others dealing with the same issues I do .Thank You that I do not feel so completely alone now. It is so nice not to have to pretend that I can handle life all the time. You know I cannot.

Thank you that BIAK came across my radar. They do so much to help our brain injury community. They have certainly made my life more manageable and given me ways to help others.

Thank You that my siblings came up with the idea for the Brain Ball. It is such a wonderful success every year. Look at how many people it brings together to help. Every year as the Brain Ball gears up, I smile knowing that my family started it all, out of their love for me.

Chapter 16

MY KINSMAN REDEEMER

May the Lord repay you for what you have done. May you be richly rewarded by the LORD, the God of Israel, under whose wings you have come to take refuge.

Ruth 2 :12

Ruth is one of the shortest books of the Old Testament. It tells the story of a young Moabite woman named Ruth, who was the daughter-in-law of Naomi, from Bethlehem of Judea. Bethlehem suffered a severe famine, causing Naomi to leave with her husband and sons for the land of Moab. There her sons both fell in love with and married Moabite women.

Naomi's husband died, and within a few years, both of her sons died also. One daughter-in-law went back to her family at Naomi's urging, but Ruth refused to leave her side. She told Naomi, *Where you go I will go, and where you stay I will stay. Your people will be my people* and *your God my God. Ruth 1:16*

So Ruth traveled back to Bethlehem with Naomi, since the famine had subsided. She went to find work at a nearby farm to provide food for herself and Naomi. The owner of that farm was a kind, generous, single man named Boaz. Boaz was in Naomi's family line as the kinsman redeemer.

The kinsman redeemer took responsibility for protecting and providing for the livelihood of the unmarried females in the family line, so Naomi orchestrated a marriage union between Ruth and Boaz, thus ensuring that he would be the kinsman redeemer for both her and Ruth.

Perhaps you are confused as to why I have told you a Bible story. It is because kinsman redeemers have been very present and active in my life.

I met with a Christian counselor a few years ago. After having me read the story of Ruth, he suggested I pray for my own kinsman redeemer. I thought he was suggesting I pray for a husband, and I knew that would take a real act of God, since I could no longer rely on my looks to attract a man. I quickly discovered that lack of mobility is not an attractive trait. Even if I tried to swing my hips, I would quickly lose my balance. Now that would turn some heads!

Since my brain injury, I had not been able to drive. My reaction time was not fast enough to drive safely in traffic, so I relied on friends or the paratransit service to take me places. When I earned my certifications as a personal trainer and group fitness instructor, I needed a reliable form of transportation to get me to the exercise classes I led at senior homes and centers all around Louisville.

That was when my four brothers stepped up to the plate. They offered to pay for a driver to take me to and from my classes, and to be available for any other errands I needed to run during the day. My drivers usually worked from 10:00 AM to 3:00 PM. In that amount of time, I could easily teach two classes, go to the health club for my own workout, and still have time for other errands like the grocery, the bank, or doctor appointments.

Not only did this give me back my independence, but it gave me wonderful new friendships with the men or women who drove me. I spent more time with my drivers than I did anyone else during the day. Because of them AND my brothers, I was able to be out in the world again, interacting with people and doing what I loved most: working out, shopping and socializing.

My four brothers Dan, John, Paul, and Andrew became my kinsman redeemers. They certainly followed in their father's footsteps, since Dad had always made himself available to help me. In his Dad sort of way, he usually just took charge and ran things for me.

When I found a newer, larger condominium in my building that I wanted to buy, the first approval that I wanted was Dad's. He met me at the new place accompanied by his real estate agent, to check the place out. He was so impressed with the condo that it only took a few minutes before he turned and said *I think you should get it, Mary. You deserve it.* Then he recommended his real estate agent.

That was just the beginning of his help. Since Dad had been my power of attorney since I returned to Louisville, he was on the phone with my banker, my stockbroker and my and his favorite handyman to get everything working as it should.

Dad seemed to take delight in watching me pick out paint colors and make decorating plans. The move consumed my life for several months, but I felt as though all I had to do was show up at the closing and sign the checks. Dad took care of most everything else. He was indeed my kinsman redeemer.

I gave my four brothers ball caps embroidered with *Kinsman Redeemer* one year for Christmas. As I was explaining the story of Ruth and Boaz, my brother John quipped that a kinsman redeemer sounded like an Old Testament *sugar daddy.* I told them I was still praying for a kinsman redeemer for weekends and social occasions. Then Paul assured me that he would keep his eye out for a Boaz for me.

Not to be outdone by the males in the family, my sister Julie often became my kinsman redeemer on weekends and after my drivers had gone home for the day. All the Varga family members are my kinsmen, and they most certainly have been my redeemers.

After I returned home at 3:00 PM, I generally spent the rest of the day and evening alone. That is when Jesus became my redeemer. Of course He was always my redeemer, but His presence became even more apparent when I was in solitude. Thanks to Him, I was never alone.

The opening scripture verse for this chapter, from Ruth 2:12, seemed most appropriate because the Lord has richly rewarded me and taken me under His wing through my kinsman redeemers. He also took away any feelings of loneliness by allowing me to feel His presence whether alone or in a crowd.

I truly believe God was showing me His favor because I was a favored daughter, always devoted to doing His will, despite the curve ball life threw me.

Dear Lord,

You do really love me! You have taken such special care of me by giving me a loving family. Thanks to the generosity of my brothers, I am able to keep the little income I make from my classes.

Through my drivers, You have given me back my independence, allowing me to make many special friends in the process.

Thank You for the most precious father a girl could ever ask for.

Help me to remember this whenever I have a 'poor me' episode.

After my mom passed on to heaven, my Dad finally started to live again when he married Martha. This is a photo of both of our families when they married.

Chapter 17

MY CHANGING WALK WITH GOD

He has shown you, O mortal, what is good. And what does the Lord require of you? To act justly and to love mercy and to walk humbly with your God.

Micah 6:8

Having been raised Roman Catholic, my siblings and I went to twelve years of Catholic elementary and high school. We went to church every Sunday. Dad took my brothers to 7:30 AM mass and Mom took my sister Julie and me to the noon mass. The girls got to sleep in, but the boys got to pick all the bakery treats from Waggoner Bakery every Sunday morning. Then they would argue over who got the sports section of the newspaper when they got home from church and the bakery. My brother Paul became adept at reading the headlines upside-down, so two could actually read at one time.

God was very much a part of our family life, as was the Catholic Church. We observed Advent and Lent with special rituals. I gave up sweets for Lent most years. When Lent was over, I gorged myself on Easter candy. We went to Confession regularly. (It has since been renamed the sacrament of Reconciliation.) I do not partake of that sacrament very often anymore. I think the Catholic Church had the right idea, though. God tells us He remembers our sins no more. When the priest absolved me of my sins, I felt the slate was really wiped clean.

We had crucifixes in most rooms of the house to testify that Jesus Christ was the first priority in our home. We had family prayer time every evening in the boys' bedroom when we were younger. A special memory for me was the night my dad tucked me in and taught me how to pray the *Hail Mary.* That was a lot of words for a five–year-old to remember. My first official prayer! I prayed it over and over in my mind.

The Catholic Church had a special adoration for the Blessed Virgin Mary, Mother of God. Mom named me Mary because I was born on one of the Blessed Mother's feast days during the Catholic calendar year. I learned to pray the rosary at a very early age. My friend Meg, who had recently joined the Catholic faith, asked me how I made a distinction between regular prayer time and praying the rosary to Mary. I see the rosary as a great intercessory prayer. I told Meg I did not pray the rosary on a daily basis, but reserved it for when I really needed to pull out *the big guns.*

High school senior retreat marked the first deepening of my faith. The retreat leaders suggested we start a journal to communicate with God. I loved writing even way back then, so I began a diary with the Lord that has continued off and on for almost forty years. Many of my conversations with God at the end of each chapter come from my past journals.

I got busy with life after college. God was always there, but I did not spend much time in prayer with Him. That all changed when I had my traumatic brain injury. I remember praying the ten *Hail Marys* on my fingers in the hospital, since I did not have a rosary with me. It seems I regressed to old, familiar prayers during that time.

Learning to pray again

After my brain injury, I wanted a closer walk with God. In my heart, I knew He had saved my life that day. I did not know how to thank Him, though. I was not sure I was even praying the right way, so I called someone whose walk with God I trusted; someone I had seen turn to God in times of difficulty. I called my brother Dan. It was an odd long-distance phone call. "Hey Dan! Can you tell me how to pray?"

Dan flew down to Little Rock that week to talk with me. He brought me his *Christian Book of Prayer/the Liturgy of the Hours.* It had prayers for Morning, Day, Evening and Night for each day of the Catholic liturgical calendar. It became the cornerstone of my prayer life, along with my copy of *God Calling.*

After being home from the hospital for a few months, I asked my mother-in-law, Bettye Jane, if I could talk with her pastor, Father Henry, at the Episcopal Church. A priest from my church had given me the anointing of the sick, formerly called *Last Rites,* when I was in a coma. I did not know him well and felt more comfortable with Father Henry, since I had been to Bettye Jane's church several times.

When I visited with Father Henry, I told him that I had never thanked God for sending me my husband, or my beautiful son. He just smiled and said, "He knows." Father Henry then suggested that Drew and I say a prayer for each other out loud at night, followed by the *Our Father.* We did that almost every night until about a month before

Drew sent me home to Louisville. Should I have seen some writing on the wall?

I also went to my first-ever Bible study in Little Rock. Ladies from other Christian denominations seemed much more comfortable and adept at studying scripture. My only exposure to God's word had been the gospels and the epistle readings from the Catholic mass. Those ladies quoted scriptures like my brothers quoted sports scores. How did they do that? Did that mean they knew God better than I did?

I was challenged enough to pull out my Bible to see what I was missing. Was that God's plan to get me to read His word? My favorite story was about Joseph in Genesis. Boy, did life throw him a curve ball! Just look what he did with it, though. My frustrations and hardships were no more than Joseph's were...just different. His walk with God was clearly deeper than my own. That challenged me too. I wanted God to walk with me like he did with Joseph, so others would know He was with me.

Joseph was our patriarch Jacob's son. He had many brothers, but Joseph was his father's favorite, being the son of Jacob's favorite wife, Rebekah. His brothers, being very jealous, sold Joseph to slave traders, after rescuing him from the pit they had thrown him into.

Joseph spent many years in prison, but he always seemed to end up in charge of things. Everyone recognized God's presence with him. Eventually, he became second in command to the Pharaoh himself. I identified so much with Joseph's unwarranted hardships. I wanted God's favor on me, too! I seemed to gloss over the fact that Joseph spent years as a slave and in prison, always remaining true to God and being of service to others.

Psalm 27:14 tells us to *Wait for the Lord; be strong and take heart and wait for the Lord.* This is a scripture verse I would do well to remember always. Sometimes it is easy to wait for circumstances to line up in the right way. Sometimes, though, especially if I have worked hard for something, I want it now! Then I start rationalizing. *It's not that I do not trust your timing, Lord, but I do not want to be lazy. If I want this so much, should I not be working or at least talking about it?* God's word tells us to wait expectantly. God meant to wait with hopeful anticipation, not to be distressed and worried about the matter. He also commanded us to wait with obedience to Him and service to others. That imperative tripped me up every time.

Now that I was disabled, what could I possibly do to serve others? I was always asking people to help me; what assistance could I possibly offer them? I kept thinking back to the priest who told me I had been given the gift of helping people honor God by helping me. My job was to be appreciative, happy and concerned about their life as they tried to help me. Once I teased my neighbor, Rick, when I knew I had gotten on his last nerve. "Just remember that you are honoring God right now!"

God's word became a daily habit for me when I was in Bible study. I always missed the guidance and direction it gave me when classes broke during the summer. Television evangelists became a regular part of my daily existence. Joyce Meyer Ministries was at the top of my list. Joyce was so sassy, sarcastic and real. She brought God to me in a way that no Catholic priest had ever done; yet my heart remained devoted to the Catholic faith. I loved all the rituals, the holy sacraments and the devotion to the Blessed Virgin Mary.

I still did not know if I was praying in a way that reached the ears of God, though. Dan had given me wonderful psalms and written prayers to the Lord, but they were still someone else's words. The writer in me wondered if God considered that plagiarism. The authors had said it so eloquently; surely God was okay with adding my "me too" to the end of it.

More prayers

When I began attending Bible Study Fellowship (BSF), our group leader gave us A.S.K. lists every week. These were the prayer requests that ladies in our small group had submitted. A.S.K. stood for Ask, Seek, and Knock. That is when I realized I was not very good at praying for others. I could not figure out what to say. *God, please bless them, direct their path, take care of their needs.* Was that enough?

When I was pressed for time, did God mind if I asked Him to bless and watch over my family, instead of listing them all by name? I have a huge family! Then I decided God just wanted to hear from me. Special time with God was always rejuvenating, but I could pray in the bathroom or at the kitchen sink, too. God just wanted to hear from me. Bible reading was time with God. Writing this book was time with God. Is that considered prayer time? I decided to call it that. Seems I have spent more time with God than I realized.

Finally going deeper

Living by myself gave me the luxury of controlling the television remote. There was no one to argue with about program selections, so I watched a lot of Christian programs. I also became a Christian inspirational book junkie.

Who was I kidding? That is not the same as communicating with the Lord. I could be eating, cleaning up the kitchen or making dinner. I was using God for background music.

A few ladies from my Bible study group went with me to see the movie *War Room.* It was the best 'How-to' on praying I have ever seen or read. I was so happy to see a movie like that in mainstream media. The acting was great, but I do not think the *War Room* will see many Academy Award nominations. So I bought the DVD and watch a few minutes of it for inspiration whenever my walk with God needs some juice.

The *War Room* is the story of a young couple having marital problems. The wife's mentor urges her to let God fight the battle for her. Regular, strategic prayer in a private room would be required.

So after a lifetime of thinking about God, wondering if He even heard my prayers, I finally began regular communications with Him in Andrew's bedroom. That was the one room in my condominium that was free from all distractions. Andrew will simply have to ignore my prayer requests all over his wall when he comes to visit. Perhaps I can get him to join me in prayer like we did when he was younger.

Identifying the enemy

The devil made me do it. I remember how Flip Wilson used to declare his innocence in Saturday Night Live skits by blaming it on the devil. I never thought Satan would bother me, though. Who was I that he would feel compelled to torment me? I assumed he only bothered important people; people who were making a difference.

Then one day my friend Tracy suggested that Satan had changed the way I looked at myself. Yes, I knew God had blessed me with looks, intelligence, accomplishments, loving family and friends. However, I believed that when others looked at me, they immediately based their opinion of me on my disabilities. I thought needing a cane or walker made me weak. I shied away from taking a stand on anything. Who would care about my position?

Tracy thought Satan was using my need for assistance to make me feel worthless. I can tell you he was doing a darn good job! So I began praying more earnestly to resist his attacks. Jesus resisted Satan with the word of God. Yeah! Now I can use my Bible concordance to locate the best scriptures for fighting the enemy.

Dear Lord,

My mind goes a thousand miles an hour, jumping from one thing to another. Please help me to slow down to hear You and acknowledge Your presence in my life. I have difficulty keeping my focus on You. I think about so many other things in prayer.

Having a special room just for praying has made all the difference in the world. I offer my prayers as a pleasing incense to You. We all like special gifts. I figure we got that from You, so I no longer worry whether You are listening or not. I offer my prayers as a gift to You. I feel more confident that You hear me.

Please help me to be attentive to Satan's maneuvers in my life. I really thought no one was concerned with my opinion anymore. The devil has really had me fooled! Thank You that you have already defeated him!

Chapter 18

<u>MOUNTAINTOP MOMENTS</u>

His master replied, 'Well done, good and faithful servant! You have been faithful with a few things; I will put you in charge of many things. Come and share your master's happiness.'

Matthew 25:21

My life has been marked by physical disability since May 1997. Despite all the hurt, frustrations and disappointments of this different life I now have, God has given me many uplifting mountaintop moments to keep me smiling and feeling blessed. These were the events where He poured his favor on me *in spite of* or even *because of* my brain injury.

The first mountaintop moment I recall was when a news anchor from a local television network asked if she could interview me for a special news segment entitled *Ordinary People, Extraordinary Lives*. The anchor, Elizabeth, had been watching me as I worked out at my health club. She was impressed with my positive outlook and dogged determination to master whatever I was trying to accomplish in my workout. I had just moved out on my own after spending two years at my parents' house. Elizabeth interviewed me in my new apartment with a cameraman taking shots of my home decorating skills. We became fast friends in the process. Our next stop was the health club to film me as I did my fitness routine. Elizabeth also got remarks from Diane, the Wellness Center president. Diane had been one of my biggest advocates since I joined.

It was very surreal to see myself on the news. Elizabeth made me sound like a real hero. "Faith, family and friends kept her going," she commented, much to my delight. Another member of my health club, whom I had never met, gave me his trophy from a 5K race he had run earlier that year. His note said that I deserved it more than him. It gave me goose bumps all over!

Another mountaintop moment that has happened every year since 2004 is the Brain Ball, with the presentation of the annual Mary Varga award. Wow! They named an award after me? What inspired the Brain Injury Alliance of Kentucky (BIAK) to do that? My family started the Brain Ball out of their love for me and their desire to help others who were facing plights similar to mine. The award was named after me, not just because I sustained a brain injury, but because of my determination to help and honor others who were also inflicted with this life-altering injury. Every year I choose another brain injury survivor who has done amazing, or even simple things to improve the lives of others. Last year's Mary Varga award winner was a United States Marine Corps Sergeant who went to work for the Wounded Warrior program after sustaining a traumatic brain injury while trying to rescue a damaged tank's crew in Afghanistan.

I am privileged to know all the details of the winner's brain injury and the challenges they have overcome to get where they are today. I get to know heroes I would not otherwise have known. I smile when I see how humbled they are to receive my award. I guess this really is a big deal. Knowing that humbles me.

More mountaintop moments

Scott is a business leader, deacon and long-time friend of the family. He and his wife JoAnn financed a scholarship in my name at my own alma mater, Assumption High School, called the *Mary Varga Life of Courage* scholarship. Every May at Assumption's Student Awards Assembly a student is chosen who exemplifies courage and a positive outlook in the face of very challenging life circumstances. Scott, JoAnn and I choose from a list of students that have been nominated by faculty or other students. It is a thrill to attend the assembly every year and see the honor and excitement in the winner we have chosen.

In May of 2012, I was also inducted into Assumption High School's Hall of Fame. I received the *Spirit Award* given to an alumna who has made a difference in the lives of others, while staying connected to the school. What a great honor! It made me feel even more connected to such a fine, Catholic high school for girls.

The mountaintop moments I have described thus far were the direct result of my sustaining a traumatic brain injury along with the kindness and attention given to me because of my plight. I try always to remember the following scripture when thinking of the kindness people have shown me. Psalm 115:1--:

Not to us, LORD, not to us but to your name be the glory, because of your love and faithfulness.

God also tells us in Revelation 2:3, *You have persevered and have endured **hardships** for my name, and have not grown weary.* I don't think these triumphant times would have been possible were it not for my faith in God and my determination to make something worthwhile out of this life-altering tragedy. It also reinforced my belief that others look out for those who are weaker or more frail than they.

Yet another mountaintop moment was born from my desire to help seniors attain a fitness level that would make it easier for them to master the demands of everyday living. I started my own business leading exercise classes for seniors to improve their muscle strength and flexibility.

Finding a name that was not already in use and under patent was a fun challenge. My brother had a friend who was a patent and trademark attorney. I first used the name ElderFit, but after a year, my attorney friend discovered a business in California with the same name. My next choice for a name was SilverStrong, but my friend suggested SilverStrength, since there were too many fitness-type businesses that already had *strong* in their name. So after a successful patent search, *SilverStrength* was born, giving a name to doing what I love.

I thought that being a business owner was meant for entrepreneurs with a keen business sense. Never did I imagine having a business doing what I love, which is exercising, while teaching a room full of eager learners. And to think I'm getting paid to do this!

Every day brings me pride and joy as I lead these SilverStrength classes. My intention is to bring the seniors I teach a better confidence in their own fitness and independent mobility. Each time I lead a class, I feel that I have truly accomplished something good and worthwhile. I have achieved daily mountaintop moments since I started my little business in 2010.

Our local newspaper did a story on my classes. The publicity brought notoriety not only to me, but to the retirement community where I taught. The ladies and men who came to class that day were glad they did. They got to see their picture in the newspaper.

My New Home

The last mountaintop moment that I will mention did not occur exclusively because of my brain injury, but because of the love and support of family and friends.

I lived in a beautiful, two-bedroom condominium for eight years. I'm a fairly neat, organized person, but over the years it was necessary to house a treadmill in my bedroom, a mini-trampoline in my dining room, a computer and filing cabinetry in my living room. Exercise equipment was in every corner of my home. I needed a bigger place!

My neighbor Rick was on the board of directors of our condominium complex. He alerted me to a larger unit going up for sale on the first floor of my building. I called the owner to arrange a time to come see it. I brought my sister Julie with me for a second opinion.

The layout was similar to my own unit, but with a third room on the main hallway that could be used as an office or work-out room. The huge great room began with a spacious kitchen with a center island, and then went on with ample square footage for both a living room and dining room. There were windows on all three sides with a large terrace that looked out at the condominium across the parking lot and neighborhoods to either side. The only thing required before I made a bid was the approval of my dad. I knew he would tell me if it was not a wise purchase. He loved it, though.

The month before my move was filled with picking paint colors, refurbishing cabinets and shopping for new pieces to fill my expanded square footage. Once the handyman, Marty, got started, there were usually one or more workers in my new condo every day. I was on Cloud 9! I usually came home to a solitary existence when I finished working. No more afternoon naps for a while. I was in constant transit between my third floor condo and the first floor condo I was moving into. I had lost five unnecessary pounds by my move date.

My sister and sisters-in-law helped me clean and stage the condo I was trying to sell to make it appear more buyer-friendly. Then all of my neighbors helped me store and move everything we could physically carry to my new unit; the movers could carry the rest. My neighbor, Rick, took charge of moving my computer and dealing with the cable company. That was a huge weight off my shoulders.

On the official moving day, my sweet dad was there unpacking my kitchen, moving things to my storage unit and bringing lunch for us all. After several hours of unpacking, Dad had to leave because his back was hurting him. I felt like a little girl again. My dad couldn't possibly be tired! He was supposed to be invincible.

Rick was the first to arrive that morning and the last to leave that evening. I then rode my scooter up to Subway to get a sandwich for dinner. It was completely dark by the time I arrived home again. My prayers were heard for sure that night!

Moving was not just a mountaintop moment, but a *coming-into-my-own* experience. I was again renewed by all the support and camaraderie from family and friends. I had a real home again. I could entertain my whole family with seating for everyone. I could live here happily for the rest of my life. It was so pretty! If my dream of being married again ever comes true, this place is certainly big enough for two. If it never happens, then I'm happy to just keep hanging with the

Lord. He tells us in Isaiah 54:5, *For your Maker is your husband. The Lord Almighty is his name.*

Dear Lord,

Thank You for giving me so many moments of encouragement to keep me going as I continue living with my disabilities and all of the challenges they present. When I look back at the mountaintop moments that You have sent me, it appears that brain injury has brought me a little fame. Help me to remember that the glory belongs to You, not me. I wouldn't even be alive to experience these moments of enchantment if You had not kept me here on earth for a reason.

You tell me in Jeremiah 29:11 that You have plans to prosper me and not to harm me, plans to give me a hope and a future. I look forward eagerly to what Your plans for me will be. I pray these mountaintop moments lead me to the wonderful plan You have for my life.

You've sent so many loving, generous people into my life. Please reward them all with Your kindness in their lives. Give me the abilities to help where I can.

James 1:2 tells us: Blessed is the one who perseveres under trial because, having stood the test, that person will receive the crown of life that the Lord has promised to those who love him. You've already given me a crown in the new home I enjoy. Let me fill that home with people who love You as they love each other.

Chapter 19
IS IT ME? IS IT THEM? DOES IT MATTER?

And no one pours new wine into old wineskins. Otherwise, the wine will burst the skins, and both the wine and the wineskins will be ruined. No, they pour new wine into new wineskins.

Mark 2:22

While I was still single and living in Louisville, I met my friend Jennifer at my apartment complex swimming pool. We became fast friends since we were both in the healthcare field, loved eating in the same restaurants, and had a real flair for fashion. Jennifer was in pharmaceutical sales, while I was still in hospital marketing. She gave me a personal perspective on the pharmaceutical industry which encouraged me to make the jump from the hospital business.

Jennifer was originally from Arkansas and knew Drew, who was later to become my ex-husband. I had an awards trip to Disney World coming up with my pharmaceutical company and planned to take my friend

Norma, since I wasn't dating anyone special at the time. Jennifer persuaded me to let her fix me up on a long-distance blind date with Drew, claiming he was one of the funniest men she had ever known. She convinced me by saying, "Come on Mare. If you don't like him, just put a cup at his feet and let him make some money for you." *Was he really that humorous that people would throw money at him?* I had to meet this guy.

I liked Drew immediately. He was a true *smart-ass*, which was my favorite kind of humor. We fell in love and married a year and a half later. At thirty-four years old, I was too old to keep dating around. If I had any hopes for a family, it was time to settle down. With Drew by my side, I figured I'd laugh all the way beyond retirement.

Drew called Jennifer after my accident and she flew down immediately. I have a very vague memory of Jennifer and her husband Will coming to see me. Apparently she had come earlier while I was still in a coma, since Drew liked to tell me how Jennifer changed my diaper for the nurses. She was a true friend.

When Jennifer heard of our recent separation, she felt horrible for both of us and somewhat responsible since she had introduced us. *"I just wanted you to take him to Disney World for your awards trip, Mary. I never thought you would end up married to him!"* Like the scripture for this chapter, was this a case of putting new wine into old wineskins? It surely did burst the wineskins. I still haven't figured out if the *new wine* was Drew or the brain injury. I just know that Drew's commitment to me did not withstand a traumatic brain injury.

On one of her visits to Louisville to see me after my divorce, Jennifer looked at me with exasperation. *"You talk as if your life before your brain injury was some type of utopia! You were driven and caring and fun, but you always had something you were struggling with. Sometimes you were a real pain in the ass! Everything had to be on your schedule and heaven forbid it should interfere with your daily run."*

Philippians 2:3 tells us "*Do nothing out of selfish ambition or vain conceit. Rather, in humility value others above yourselves.*" According to Jennifer, selflessness was not one of my personality traits. Unfortunately my selfishness became even more apparent after my brain injury and subsequent disabilities. I had nothing else to do all day but think about myself.

This personality flaw became most obvious in my relationships with family members. I was always asking them to do something for me that I could no longer do myself. Was I demanding? I'm sure they thought I was. My dad began to answer my phone calls with *"Yes, Mary"* as if saying, *"What do you want now?"* I was heartsick that the family that carried me through my whole horrific ordeal now saw me as someone who always called needing something.

In the chapter *Ashamed of My Physical Self*, I told you that Andrew once told me, "Everybody loves you Mommy, but nobody wants to fool with you." Only my son had the brutal honesty to say what everyone else was thinking. Of course they weren't going to tell their daughter or sister they didn't want to fool with her. They just didn't include me in their daily lives.

Who am I kidding, though? I never felt the urge to be a daily part of my family's lives. I was always an independent loner who adored her family and loved running into them or seeing them at times that were convenient for me. I hadn't seen them daily since we lived together as children.

I had lost my little family when Drew divorced me. I'm just now realizing how critical those first few years living with Mom and Dad were to me. I was physically not able to live on my own yet, but emotionally, it was vital that I be with people that loved and cared for me.

Psalm32:7 says of the Lord, *You are my hiding place; you will **protect** me from trouble and surround me with songs of deliverance.* Jesus was giving me protection through my family. They watched over me constantly when I could not do for myself. Never did I hear a complaint of what they were sacrificing to take care of me.

As I became more independent, they could loosen their grip on me. Mom and Dad remained my constants, though. That usually included dinner three or four nights a week. It wasn't until my mother died in 2004 that I realized just how much I relied on her attention and affection. She made me feel like the most important person in her life. I miss her especially when I'm sick. Living alone is hard when you're sick. I wanted my mom there to bring me cokes and aspirin and play movies for me.

When Dad remarried and moved, I could no longer walk to his house for dinner. Since Dad was my connection with the rest of the family, I began feeling more isolated. I could certainly have called them, but was afraid they wouldn't want to hear from me or try to understand my goofy voice. Sometimes, I just didn't want to put forth the effort.

They all had busy lives with kids, work and social engagements. I used to have a life like that. I wasn't envious of them, but always proud of them. Their lack of interest in my life added to my feeling of being completely insignificant. *What could I possibly offer them? I couldn't even drive over for a visit. If I could, what would I even talk about?* All I ever seemed to do was work out and shop. It appears I lost my ability to converse after my brain injury.

I was totally focused on making myself better. It was my full-time occupation. I remember now what my sister Julie told me once. *People like to talk about themselves, so ask a lot of questions.* Asking questions required taking my mind off of myself for a minute. It required being curious about someone besides myself. I had become so blamed selfish! Could I even do it?

That changed somewhat when I started working. I was out in the world again, connecting with people. I put on my happy face for several hours each day. After a while, I started bringing that happiness home with me, too. God tells us in Philippians 2:3, *Do nothing out of selfish ambition or vain conceit. Rather, in humility value others above yourselves.*

Doing for others really does bring more fulfillment. Thankfully, the business I've created caters to other people's needs. I know I inspire them by doing things that require extra effort. Since walking steadily falls into that category, I get to inspire people all day long!

Since my brain injury, God has placed many kind and helpful people in my life. Sometimes they seem to take on helping me as a project. I know then that God is smiling at them and me. After several months, though, they seem to lose their steam. Being in constant contact with a disabled person has to be exhausting. They are always helping me, which I hope makes them feel good.

Is there something I could do to keep them engaged? Am I saying something wrong? Not enough, or too much? My neighbor Rick told me I sometimes talk *curtly.* I wasn't sure what the definition of that word was, but my mom used to tell me sometimes to stop *being so curt!* I thought she was telling me not to be a *smart-ass.* Apparently, I still have that tendency.

All these years I thought friends just got tired of helping me physically maneuver through life. Has it been me all along? I know I'm bullheaded, always trying to do things myself; then beating myself up when I can't. I walk a fine line between being overly grateful and assuming others are going to take care of me. No one wants to feel taken advantage of, even by a nice little disabled lady.

I think the heart of this issue is that I have never really accepted the fact that I am disabled and that there are things I cannot physically do, no matter how I try. The fact that I have a brain injury makes me very touchy if my intelligence is ever questioned. When people try to over-explain things to me, I need to just smile and laugh it off instead of giving them a *curt* response.

I never fully grasped what discrimination was until I became a disabled person. I know now how it feels to be treated differently than others, or have your opinion discounted or ignored. On the flip side, though, I get to see the kindness and generosity in people who are trying to make life easier or more manageable for me.

If the *new wine* is my new life with disabilities, I've been trying for over eighteen years to fit it into the *old wineskins* of the life I had before my brain injury. I've seen those wineskins burst many times as I tried to pretend that my life hasn't been changed. Perhaps it's time to get some new wineskins. In Deuteronomy 6:2 God tells us, *You have stayed long enough at this mountain.* I can't change my disabilities; only God can do that. It's time to stop putting life on hold until I conquer my limitations and start being a regular person again.

The ironic thing is that I have always striven to be more than just a regular Joe. I wanted to be unique and special. One of my favorite scriptures is Isaiah 43:19, *See, I am doing a new thing! Now it springs up; do you not perceive it? I am making a way in the wilderness and streams in the wasteland.* This new life can include all those I held dear before while still embracing the special life I have now.

Is it me? Is it them? Does it matter? There are probably numerous misconceptions on all our parts, but the truth is that it really doesn't matter. We are all a part of God's family and need to celebrate the unique talents or contributions that each of us brings to the table.

Dear Lord,

Thank You for your patience and understanding with all the new things I'm trying to deal with since becoming disabled. They're really not even new anymore. It's been over eighteen years! Think it's time for me to embrace a new way of living?

I spend so much time alone, it's easy to get busy and not think of others or their concerns. Please continue to help me conquer my selfishness.

I know this new life has to include You and I'm so grateful I've become so close to You over the years. So many times I've felt like You were the only one who understood me. Please enlarge my heart for all the family and friends You've placed in my life. Give me the same patience and compassion for them that they have always shown for me.

Chapter 20

HUMILITY AND THE POWER OF FORGIVENESS

Humble yourselves, therefore, under God's mighty hand, that he may lift you up in due time.

1 Peter 5:6

Being humble is defined as having or showing a consciousness of one's shortcomings. I was certainly cognizant of my physical deficits, but did I display awareness of them? When I absolutely had to I did, but I usually moved about as if everything was normal. My walking gait and lack of good balance sometimes caused me to appear as if I was drunk, or at least struggling. When concerned bystanders asked, "Do you need some help?" I would quickly respond, "No, thank you. I'm fine."

I would walk away irritated at myself for looking so *needy*. I thought I was walking pretty well, but clearly I still looked deficient in some way. This was my new *normal*. I hated that I appeared different from everyone else, yet I kept pretending that I moved about just like they did.

Proverbs 3:34 tells us, *God opposes the proud but shows favor to the humble.* I didn't think I was being proud. I just wanted to appear normal. I've often questioned whether or not I should use a walker to get around. I've told you before how much I abhor them, but would others feel better about my personal safety if I used one? I do use a walker when traveling long distances, but walk without one at other times. Not having to fool with carting a walker seemed to make everyone, myself included, more comfortable.

Putting my pride aside, it is easier and safer to walk with a walker, but it throws my body out of alignment because I lean forward to push the walker. My body naturally leans forward to protect my balance, but I call it my *walker posture,* because using a walker just magnifies the posture problem.

There are times I think Jesus wants me to put the walker aside and keep pushing. Continuously walking without a walker makes it feel easier and more natural. It also makes me slow, which is a problem for impatient people. I'm an impatient person, so I get aggravated with my own pokey speed.

Did Jesus want me to look like a cripple? Did he want me to look unattractive and weak? Of course He didn't! He did want me to humble myself before His mighty hand, though. This has become the *thorn in my flesh* that the apostle Paul spoke of in 2 Corinthians 12:7, *Therefore, in order to keep me from becoming conceited, I was given a thorn in my flesh, a messenger of Satan, to torment me.* The Lord then tells Paul in 2 Corinthians 12:9, *My grace is sufficient for you, for my power is made perfect in weakness.*

So I figure that I have a lot of God's power resting on me. That gives me comfort whenever I'm embarrassed because I need a walker to move quickly. I do understand the power of weakness. I've said before that my immobility seems to bring out the kindness and graciousness in people. I'm especially complimented when someone tells me I'm too fit and attractive to walk with *one of those things.*

Will anyone ever consider me attractive and sexy again? It's difficult to pull that look off when you're encaged in a metal walker. I suppose I should be grateful that I will never have to be concerned again that someone is just physically attracted to me. Is it even possible that someone could be attracted to me? I think I'm what others refer to as "someone who comes with a lot of baggage."

So I do indeed humble myself under the mighty hand of God. He knows the baggage I carry and how to keep me happy and hopeful whatever my situation is in this life. I still call on Him daily to help me make peace with my physical deficiencies and with my lack of companionship.

The Power of Forgiveness

Mark 11:25

*And when you stand praying, if you hold anything against anyone, **forgive** them, so that your Father in heaven may **forgive** you your sins."*

Have I forgiven the teenage boy who T-boned my car in 1997, causing my brain injury? I don't honestly think I was ever mad at him. I have no memory of the accident and have always considered it a case of being in the wrong place at the wrong time.

That teenager would be close to forty years old now. I wonder what he was thinking on that day. What impact did the accident have on his life? Did his parents ground him for wrecking the car? Did he have any concept of how it impacted my life? I'm going to add him to my prayer list, asking God to take away any feelings of guilt he may have. As far as I know, though, it was just an inconvenient day in his young life.

There was never an issue of extending forgiveness to that nameless young man. I suppose Drew might remember his name, or I could always look at the police report. The truth is that it really didn't matter. He was not legally at fault since he had no stop sign. That intersection, interestingly, is now a four-way stop. Was I responsible for that change in road signage?

Could I ever forgive Drew for divorcing me and taking my son from me? There was a time when I thought that was impossible. He had completely changed the course of my life. In the chapter entitled Being a Mother: Teenager and Young Adult, I describe how I finally forgave Drew. Putting that part of my life behind me gave me a great feeling of peace.

I also needed to show mercy to all the family and friends who have treated me differently because of the physical limitations I received in the accident. In the beginning, their care and concern for me was touching and greatly appreciated. Now it just hurts my feelings when I'm excluded from things because of my slowness and disabilities.

How do I react when someone is slowing me down? It frustrates me and makes me not want to be around them. It also makes me think again of ten-year-old Andrew's comment, "Everybody loves you, Mommy, but nobody wants to fool with you."

My disabilities have changed how I approach everything in life. They have also changed the way others approach me. It is not my fault or theirs; life is just different now. My family and friends still love me and I still love them. I truly forgive them for not wanting to be around me. Sometimes, if I could get away from me, I would.

When Peter was talking with Jesus in Matthew 18:21-22 he asked, "Lord, how many times shall I forgive my brother or sister who sins against me? Up to seven times?"Jesus answered, "I tell you, not seven times, but seventy times seven."

So, because the Lord commands it, I will continue to forgive others when they treat me differently, either discounting my opinion or ignoring me. I honestly never mind the time I spend by myself, but rather look forward to it. When I get aggravated with myself, I feel very fortunate that others aren't around to be aggravated too. I believe the Lord has given me this interruption in my life to reflect on the talents and gifts I still possess that could be used to help other people, as they have helped me. If I take my mind off of myself for a minute, it also gives me the opportunity to revel in all He has done for me through family, friends and multiple life miracles.

Dear Lord,

Thank You for finally letting me see the power of forgiveness. It is what You command us to do for each other, but I never realized what u weight it would take off my shoulders. I don't hurt anyone but myself by being angry. My offender probably hasn't given their words or actions a second thought.

You tell us in Luke 6:37, "Do not judge, and you will not be judged. Do not condemn, and you will not be condemned. Forgive, and you will be forgiven." I never expected this command to come with such a feeling of joy and relief. Please remind me of that when I feel myself getting aggravated with life.

Chapter 21

SUFFERING: IT'S PART OF LIFE

Now if we are children, then we are heirs—heirs of God and co-heirs with Christ, if indeed we share in his sufferings in order that we may also share in his glory.

Romans 8:17

My initial, life-threatening suffering was almost two decades ago. God was with me then and has walked with me through the many years I have journeyed this dark tunnel of brain injury and disability. My temperament and behavior during those early days has now become a legend of sorts. The famous quote, "This too shall pass" is clearly evident in the reactions of family and friends to my 1997 trauma.

My brother Paul once commented that life in the Varga family could be divided into *Life before Mary's accident* and *Life since Mary's accident*. This trauma had not just affected my life, but the lives of everyone who was close to me. In true Varga fashion, though, *Life since Mary's accident* was sometimes told with a humorous note. Refer to the chapter *Entering the Tunnel* where I talk about Michele, milkshakes and my potty mouth. I see it as a sign of family healing that we could all look back at that time and laugh.

The fact that we can laugh at it now in no way diminishes suffering's effect on all of our lives, particularly mine. Paul tells us in Romans 5:3-4, *Not only so, but we also glory in our sufferings, because we know that suffering produces perseverance; perseverance, character; and character, hope.* The agony of existing in a disabled body propelled my determination and perseverance to a new level.

Getting from *perseverance* to *character* took me a few more years and is still evolving. That character developed as I struggled to overcome physical challenges and finally succeeded. That brought forth a desire to help others who grappled with similar obstacles. That produced a real sense of joy in bringing hope and encouragement to others.

I just described the feelings associated with overcoming my physical challenges and the contentment that comes from reaching out to others. What about my emotional suffering? There has been an abundance of that since my brain injury.

You probably think I'm referring to my divorce and the abandonment I felt. I suffered for many years, and still do somewhat, with not being able to share in my son's trials and triumphs. I was indeed robbed of Andrew's childhood. Little Rock is a long way away. I still get heartsick at all I'm missing.

I know Andrew loves me, but it makes me feel unimportant that he feels no need to share his feelings with me. So I pray for him...earnestly. I also pray that his father and stepmother will guide him in the right direction.

My emotional suffering also comes in the form of being different from others. Disabled or handicapped individuals are now referred to as people with *special needs*. I really didn't want to be that special, I swear! I don't like having my walking gait evaluated. I don't like having my intelligence questioned because I speak so laboriously. I miss having men look at me just because I'm cute and not because I'm disabled.

Can I be trusted with the suffering God has entrusted to me? I'm not always sure what God wants me to do. I know that sometimes it's best to not react to difficulties. That's so hard, though. I always feel the need to do something—anything. So I pray for wisdom every day.

I also pray to keep my big mouth shut. Suffering people feel justified in talking about their woes. I've been guilty of this in attempting to get it off my chest and feel better. Is that really what I was attempting to do, though? Was I not trying to put blame on someone or something else for my lot in life?

James 3:2 tells us, *We all stumble in many ways. Anyone who is never at fault in what they say is perfect, able to keep their whole body in check.* According to the Bible, I was certainly far from perfect. I've been negative, complaining and judgmental. Did my suffering exonerate me? No! My complaining was a sin!

I do believe that God is a loving father who desires the best for all His family. He saved my life and has allowed me to see His love for me in the words and actions of people who have helped me to manage my new life as a disabled person. I believe God wants to see what I can accomplish for Him in this new life.

Suffering teaches and molds character like nothing else can do. It has certainly made me more patient and compassionate with others. It's given me a whole new perspective on the challenges many face with ambulating their body. It has also magnified the one quality that God endowed me with at a very early age. That quality is strength.

Once I put my mind to something, it was very difficult to get me off course in achieving my goal. I readily accepted additional work, effort, and even embarrassment if I believed it was necessary to accomplish the task at hand. In my disabled world, sometimes that meant the extra energy and effort needed to walk unassisted. Other times, it meant the embarrassment of walking with a walker to feel steady. Yes, after two decades, using a walker is still an embarrassment to me. Isn't embarrassment another form of suffering?

On a humorous note, suffering actually rewrote a chapter in my life. Articles have been written describing what I lost after my brain injury. One article read, "Varga, once a competitive runner..." In the twenty plus years that I ran, I paid the entry fee and got the T-shirt from many local road races and two New York City marathons. I ran an eight and a half minute mile. After a traumatic brain injury, that seemed to be enough to qualify me as a competitive distance runner!

The abundant life that Jesus offers us is not a life free of hardships. So I will accept, sometimes begrudgingly, the hardships that come with a disabled life. My spiritual life has flourished in the midst of all my physical difficulties. No matter the disgust I feel with my physical performance, I know that Jesus loves me and is pleased with my efforts. I don't think my spiritual muscle would be as strong today without the suffering that has increased my perseverance and determination. It has surely brought me closer to God. I have a new perspective now on the value of personal suffering. God allows it in our lives to grow us.

I will always want to avoid it, but suffering is a part of our lives as human beings. I also believe that staying in close communication with God can make the unavoidable a bearable and even learning experience for us. Then we can take the lessons we've learned and use them to help others that are suffering.

Dear Lord,

What a journey we have made together. You have given me so much courage and strength in this odd predicament. Many would have crumbled, but I felt You with me every step of the way. You have blessed me with unbelievable family and friends, and most importantly a spirit to never give up.

I still pray for a miracle to restore my balance and voice. Please let me be the miracle that helps others who have struggled as I have.

Thank you for the good things You have in store for my life. I smile when I think of the future You have prepared for me.

Andrew and I at a recent Brain Ball.

Chapter 22

DO I REALLY WANT A MAN IN MY LIFE?

They help each other and say to their companions, "Be strong!"

Isaiah 41:6

I have been without male companionship for over nineteen years. I certainly didn't have any bad feelings about men because of my divorce. I didn't even have any hard feelings about Drew sending me back to Louisville. I just felt that my luck had run out.

Whether intentionally or not, Drew made me feel like less of a person after my brain injury. I used to tease that he thought I was retarded. His misconceptions about brain injury affected me greatly. I used to have hard feelings about that. He never solicited or listened to my opinion anymore. His primary job as a husband seemed to be keeping me comfortable and out of the way. I'm not sure if he thought I was even capable of a rational thought.

All he knew was that his cute, athletic wife was now physically disabled. My helpless, erratic behavior when coming out of my coma must have been traumatic for him. That impression of me seemed to stick in his mind. I quickly became someone that had to be taken care of, since I could not do it myself. One of his reasons for divorcing me was because he grew tired of taking care of two babies, both Andrew and me.

When I returned to Louisville, improving my physical deficits became my all-consuming passion. My family supported all of my efforts, whether physical therapy, speech therapy, or countless hours of exercising and walking. I'm not sure they thought I was making any improvement, but they knew it made me feel more in control of my predicament.

The infamous words of my then ten-year-old son remained burned in my memory and my outlook. "Everybody loves you Mommy, but nobody wants to fool with you." This honest proclamation forever colored my impression of how other people viewed me. That impression certainly included men.

In order to protect myself, I tried not to need anyone, either. That's hard when you can't reach things on the top shelf and don't have the balance to stand on a stool. So I did need to allow a few strong, able bodies into my world. Still, aside from needing reliable transportation, I became as totally independent as possible.

In the chapter entitled *My Kinsmen Redeemers,* I spoke of the eternal gratitude I had that my four brothers helped me pay for drivers that enabled me to work and participate in life without a car. I also spoke of my father's love for me as he orchestrated all the necessary steps to move me into the beautiful condominium I now call home. My kinsman redeemers had given me all the prerequisites needed to live a contented life on my own.

So, technically, I didn't need a man in my life for financial reasons or even for transportation. When I thanked my family for being my kinsmen redeemers, I told them I would keep praying for a kinsman redeemer for holidays and social occasions. Those were the two times that made me feel most alone. Still feeling self-conscious about how I moved, I also reasoned that having a man by my side would make my balance issue more manageable. A man could hold my hand to steady me and others would just think he was being affectionate.

I have found that being on my own for almost two decades came with many advantages. I could make my own schedule without considering its impact on someone else. I could do what I wanted when I wanted to unless transportation was involved. I could spend the whole afternoon writing without being concerned about how it would affect someone else. I could eat when I wanted, watch television when I wanted, and go to bed when I wanted.

God tells us in Genesis 2:8, *It is not good for the man to be alone. I will make a helper suitable for him.* Was God putting me on the black list? I couldn't physically help anyone. I could certainly be a help if someone was willing to move at my slow pace, but who would that be? Did God have someone with infinite patience and compassion waiting for me?

What if it's the woman who needs the helper? I certainly needed assistance on a daily basis, but once I got it, I was content to be on my own again. It wasn't always that way, but I have grown accustomed to spending much time by myself. I just assume that no one wants to spend hours of time with a disabled lady. So I've learned to be content by myself. I never really feel alone, anyway. I know that Jesus is just a breath or a thought away.

God also tells us in 1 Corinthians 8-9, *Now to the unmarried and the widows I say: It is good for them to stay unmarried, as I do. But if they cannot control themselves, they should marry, for it is better to marry than to burn with passion.* I don't seem to have circumstances that make me burn with passion these days, so I suppose I'll stay single until I do. A date for dinner or a movie would be nice, though. I suppose that's why God gave us girlfriends.

I'm really not searching for a male companion. I understand that I come with a lot of baggage. It takes more than a pretty face to keep someone attracted to you, so I keep a large register of folks to call when I need help, or simply companionship.

I don't think I'm a good candidate for online dating sites, either. I can make myself look really good on paper. I move around with such effort and difficulty, though, that meeting me in person would give a man a completely different impression of me. Or maybe I'm just afraid of being rejected.

I would like a soulmate in my life. I truly enjoy being part of a couple. I want someone that I can encourage and experience things with; to share my strength with. I want a man who will support and expand my walk with God. I want someone to go to family dinners with; to laugh with; to cry with.

For now, though, I'm leaving that concern in God's hands. He knows my heart. I'll just keep focusing on the activities I know have God's seal of approval, like running my little fitness business. Then if something should happen on the romantic scene, I will already be a content, independent, and joyful person. With or without a man, I know that's what God wants for me.

Dear Lord,

You know I've always dreamed of being married again. No one else seems to be concerned that I'm by myself, as long as I can take care of myself. I miss the personal attention I received when I was so needy.

I have prayed and striven for independence for so many years, but independence can come with loneliness too. Attracting a man is difficult with the way I walk and talk. Do I even want a man in my life? I have my life structured to include work, friends, and time with You. I really like being by myself. Please don't let me walk away from opportunity just because it doesn't fit in my tidy schedule.

I'm leaving this one with You, Lord. I know how much You love me. I've identified my whole life with the Varga family, but I'm definitely the black sheep of that accomplished group. They've loved and cared for me in amazing ways, but I've grown weary of being their "poster child". Please bring my miraculous healing so I can just be one of the gang again. Please give me a family of my own again. Then Andrew can have a stepdad.

Kicking off the Brain Ball (2016)...

Chapter 23
WRITING FOR GOD

See, I am doing a new thing! Now it springs up; do you not perceive it? I am making a way in the wilderness and streams in the wasteland.

Isaiah 43:19

My whole family has been blessed with an incredible talent for putting their thoughts in writing. Is that genetic or the byproduct of our upbringing? Whatever the reason, I was bitten by the writing bug from an early age. I chose journalism as a college major until I discovered that course of study was more about reporting facts and figures. I wanted to write creatively.

As I mentioned in the Introduction, I have been journaling with God since my senior year in high school. Since my brain injury in 1997, friends have encouraged me to write my story. Perhaps it's time to start writing about God and all the marvelous ways He has worked in my life, instead of just writing to Him.

My friend, also a Mary, has been very instrumental in my desire to write for God. Mary and I met when we were in the same small group in Bible Study Fellowship (BSF). She suggested I accompany her to a Louisville Christian Writers (LCW) meeting.

I was very intimidated, yet hopeful at first. This was a room full of authors, publishers, and editors. I was a handicapped lady with a funny voice and no published work. I immediately assumed they thought the worst of me, but I wanted to learn all the tricks of the trade.

Then something unexpected happened. We prayed and worshipped God together. I expected that in church, or at Bible study; I never expected it at a meeting of writers. This was another example for me of how God shows up in every aspect of life. He is not confined by the walls of a church. It was so refreshing to hear others pray and talk about God outside of Sunday morning services or Bible study. I hadn't been a part of this kind of Christian fellowship since I graduated from a Catholic high school.

LCW has been very instrumental to me in writing this book. The members critiqued most of the chapters of my story, making sure that my grammar, punctuation and verb tense were appropriate. They have also helped by telling me what topics in my story they would be interested in knowing more about. As a reader, they tell me what issues would prompt them to keep reading.

Jesus tells us in Luke 4:43, *"I must proclaim the good news of the kingdom of God to the other towns also, because that is why I was sent."* As followers of Jesus, we have the same responsibility. If my writing can bring souls to God, then what an honor and a humbling experience this is for me. Jesus came to earth to announce God's kingdom to all who would listen. My prayer is that my story will help you identify ways the Lord has been present and active in your life.

I believe that Jesus has called me to share my journey in recovery to reach out to others who are facing difficult life circumstances. Perhaps you have been through a very trying and testing time, or someone you love is going through a challenge right now. I pray that my words give you hope and comfort that God is controlling your final outcome.

Writing this book has been very therapeutic for me. I'm able to focus on the many blessings God has provided as I've journeyed through my brain injury. Our mission as Christians is to bring God glory for all He is and all He has accomplished in our lives. He has been the light through this dark tunnel I call physical disability. I should shout from the rooftops for all God has done for me. More importantly, I honor and praise Him for all that He is!

I've entitled this book *The Light Through My Tunnel.* My main desire has been to show you the infinite ways Jesus has stayed by my side and sometimes even carried me through my new life as a brain injury survivor. He's given me family to cherish, wonderful new friends, and dear old ones.

I was raised to be a kind, helpful, and truthful Catholic Christian, but evangelizing was never something I was taught to strive for. The very word, *evangelizing,* brought forth an image of the Jehovah's Witnesses that used to knock at our front door asking for money *in God's name.* I've never been a natural fundraiser or evangelist. I have, however, always spoken very comfortably about how God has shown His love and favor for me and my family.

My intent in telling my story is to reflect all the ways that God has shown Himself in my long and still-continuing struggle with brain injury recovery. I haven't yet received a miraculous physical healing, but I've developed a love and trust of God's infinite wisdom. Writing for God is my way of bragging about all He has done to bring me closer and closer to Him.

Dear Lord,

What an awesome and growing experience it has been to write for you. I may not be perfected yet in spreading your word, but writing for you has really pointed me in the right direction. I have to admit that putting words on paper is much more comfortable for me than acknowledging your work in person. Please give me the grace to do that when it's appropriate.

You have truly opened my mind and heart to look for even more ways that you are acting in my life and in the lives of others. LCW tells me to praise you through my writing.

Please accept this memoir as pleasing incense offered up to you from one of your devoted daughters.

EPILOGUE

Look! God's dwelling place is now among the people, and he will dwell with them. They will be his people, and God himself will be with them and be their God. He will wipe every tear from their eyes. There will be no more death or mourning or crying or pain, for the old order of things has passed away.

Revelation 213-4

While trying to reach the coveted *normal* life I was striving for, it occurred to me how my life had been blessed by my traumatic brain injury. My misfortunes, especially my mobility challenges, gave me the opportunity to impact so many lives that I would not have touched otherwise. My efforts to improve my balance and gait allowed me to inspire those who saw me.

The most valuable outcome of my tragedy was the immense boost it gave to my Christian walk. Jesus became real to me in ways I never imagined.

May 10, 1997 completely changed the course of my life. God was a part of my life before my accident; now He has become the center of my existence and the compass that steers me through all the trials and triumphs of my disabled life.

Matthew 6:33 says, *But seek first his kingdom and his righteousness, and all these things will be given to you as well.* After a lifetime of trying to do everything on my own, it took the challenges of my brain-injured life to finally get me to give it all to Him. It took me the better part of twenty years to do that. As I said in my introduction, I've been a resistant learner.

I find much hope in James 1:12, where we're told, *Blessed is the man who remains steadfast under trial, for when he has stood the test he will receive the crown of life, which God has promised to those who love him.* God has given me so many crowns in my journey to recovery in the form of family, friends, and mentors who have loved and guided me. He has let me experience the joy of overcoming personal challenges and helping others to overcome their obstacles.

Many of the pathways in my brain have been severed. I praise and thank God always that I retained my personality and intellect. The human brain is capable of forming new pathways to accomplish skills that were lost. So, who knows? I may run again in my earthly life.

I lost my balance, my coordination and my voice as a result of my head trauma. I lost the opportunity to raise my son. I lost the ability to keep pace with my family and friends. They have all understood and loved me anyway.

I will never know many of the treasures of being a mother to a growing son. I am confident that Andrew and I will have a stronger relationship as he becomes a young adult and faces the trials and pressures of living in an imperfect world. Then Mom will finally have some sage advice!

It is a true statement that life after a brain injury will be different, but can still be a very good life. Survivors of trauma gain a new perspective on God's love and influence in their life. Regardless of what I have lost, I have a new dedication to enjoying what I have and reaching out to others in fellowship and love.

2 Corinthians 4:17-18 tells us, *For our light and momentary troubles are achieving for us an eternal glory that far outweighs them all. So we fix our eyes not on what is seen, but on what is unseen, since what is seen is temporary, but what is unseen is eternal.* Since my time on earth is just a training ground for eternity with Jesus, I look forward with hope to that remarkable time when all of my disabilities will vanish and my only concern will be how best to praise God that day.

While I'm still here on earth, I take comfort in knowing my friends and family always have my back. All day and every day, I'm certain that Jesus has my back. Someday I will live with him eternally with all of my fears erased.

In the meantime, I'll strive to make something marvelous and valuable of my life here on earth. And yes, I will continue to pray for a medical breakthrough.

SCRIPTURE APPENDIX

While I was writing this memoir, I kept a log of inspiring scripture passages to begin each chapter. As I continued writing, I found I was using multiple Bible passages throughout the chapters. Here's a listing of Bible verses that I could not fit into my story but are nonetheless very meaningful for purposes of my life walk, and probably yours, too!

All of these verses were taken from the New International Version (NIV) of the Holy Bible.

Showing Kindness:

Be kind and compassionate to one another, forgiving each other, just as in Christ God forgave you.
Ephesians 4:32

Carry each other's burdens, and in this way you will fulfill the law of Christ.
Galatians 6:2

May these words of my mouth and this meditation of my heart be pleasing in your sight, Lord, my Rock and my Redeemer.
Psalm 19:14

In your anger do not sin. Do not let the sun go down while you are angry.
Ephesians 4:26

Trusting God's Timing:

Wait for the Lord; be strong and take heart and wait for the Lord.
Psalm 27:14

Have I not commanded you? Be strong and courageous. Do not be afraid; do not be discouraged, for the Lord you God will be with you wherever you go.
Joshua 1:9

See, I have refined you, though not as silver; I have tested you in the furnace of affliction.
Isaiah 48:10

May the God of hope fill you with all joy and peace as you trust in him, so that you may overflow with hope by the power of the Holy Spirit.
Romans 15:13

Now faith is confidence in what we hope for and assurance about what we do not see.
Hebrews 11:1

Consider him who endured such opposition from sinners, so that you will not grow weary and lose heart.
Hebrews 12:3

Therefore, we do not lose heart. Though outwardly we are wasting away, yet inwardly we are being renewed day by day.
2 Corinthians 4:16

<u>Purpose of Trust:</u>

For our light and momentary troubles are achieving for us an eternal glory that far outweighs them all.
2 Corinthians 4:17

There is no fear in love. But perfect love drives out fear.
1 John 4:18

Do not be anxious about anything, but in every situation, by prayer and petition, with thanksgiving, present your requests to God.
Philippians 4:6

So do not fear, for I am with you; do not be dismayed, for I am your God. I will strengthen you and help you; I will uphold you with my righteous right hand.
Isaiah 43:10

God's Providence:

In Him was life, and that life was the light of all mankind. The light shines in the darkness, and the darkness has not overcome it.
John 1:4-5

Ask and it will be given to you; seek and you will find; knock and the door will be opened to you.
Matthew 7:7

I am the Lord, and there is no other; apart from me there is no God. I will strengthen you, though you have not acknowledged me.
Isaiah 45:5

Commit your work to the Lord, and your plans will be established.
Proverbs 16:3

With your help I can advance against a troop; with my God I can scale a wall.
Psalm 18:29

Create in me a pure heart, O God, and renew a steadfast spirit within me.
Psalm 51:10

Now to him who is able to do immeasurably more than all we ask or imagine, according to his power that is at work within us...
Ephesians 3:20

Finally, be strong in the Lord and in his mighty power.
Ephesians 6:10

For I know the plans I have for you, declares the Lord, plans for welfare and not for evil, to give you a future and a hope.
Jeremiah 29:11

But those who hope in the Lord will renew their strength. They will soar on wings like eagles; they will run and not grow weary, they will walk and not be faint.
Isaiah 40:31

God's Goodness:

I can do all this through Him who gives me strength.
Philippians 4:13

You, Lord, keep my lamp burning; my God turns my darkness into light.
Psalm 18:28

Overcoming Trials:

But He said to me, "My grace is sufficient for you, for my power is made perfect in weakness." Therefore I will boast all the more gladly about my weaknesses, so that Christ's power may rest on me.
2 Corinthians 12:9

Be joyful in hope, patient in affliction, faithful in prayer.
Romans 12:12

Therefore, strengthen your feeble arms and weak knees. Make level paths for your feet, so that the lame may not be disabled, but rather healed.
Hebrews 12:12-13

Not only so, but we also glory in our sufferings, because we know that suffering produces perseverance; perseverance, character; and character, hope.
Romans 5:3-4

Loving Others:

For if you forgive other people when they sin against you, your heavenly Father will also forgive you.
Matthew 6:14

Do nothing out of selfish ambition or vain conceit. Rather in humility value others above
yourselves, not looking to your own interests but each of you to the interests of others.
Philippians 2:3-4

A new command I give you: Love one another. As I have loved you, so you must love one another.
John 13:4

Keeping God's Commands:

Do not be conformed to this world, but be transformed by the renewal of your mind, that by testing you may discern what is the will of God, what is good and acceptable and perfect.
Romans 12:2

Do not let wisdom and understanding out of your sight, preserve sound judgment and discretion; they will be life for you, an ornament to grace your neck.
Proverbs 3:21-22

Rather, clothe yourselves with the Lord Jesus Christ, and do not think about how to gratify the desires of the flesh.
Romans 5:3-4

Give thanks in all circumstances; for this is God's will for you in Christ Jesus.
1 Thessalonians 5:18

God's Protection:

The name of the Lord is a fortified tower; the righteous run to it and are safe.
Proverbs 18:10

I will go before you and will level the mountains; I will break down gates of bronze and cut through bars of iron.
Isaiah 41:10

Author Biography

Mary Varga is the survivor of a traumatic brain injury in 1997 that left her with a balance disability and slight speech impairment. Despite her mobility challenges, Mary is an ACSM Certified Personal Trainer and a Fitour Certified Senior Fitness Instructor. She owns a business called *SilverStrength®,* leading exercise classes for seniors in Louisville, Kentucky. She's on the board of directors of the Brain Injury Alliance of Kentucky (BIAK), presenting the Mary Varga Award every year at their annual gala, the Brain Ball.

Mary is also a member of Louisville Christian Writers (LCW) and attends weekly Bible Study at Bible Study Fellowship (BSF).

A University of Kentucky graduate, Mary lives in her hometown of Louisville, Kentucky. Mary has one son, grown and studying at college. Mary comes from a family of origin of eight and the good Lord has seen fit to increase them greatly.

Made in the USA
Lexington, KY
28 September 2017